TRUTH BEING BONDAGE

MO
ABBIE

TRUTH BEING BONDAGE

A MEMOIR

Fortified One

CONTENTS

Dedication
vii

1 — Is It Me
1

2 — The Home I Remember
5

3 — We Roll
12

4 — Lifting the Veil
26

5 — A Crack in the Foundation
34

6 — Her Reasoning, His Stress
45

7 — Life Split
49

8 — Protection
61

9 — Heavy Angst
74

10 — Playing the Background
80

CONTENTS

11 — Uncovered Memory
87

12 — Who Knew, Who Knows
101

13 — Misinterpretation of Men
111

14 — Life is an Experience, You Must Be Present to Live
122

15 — Outlook & Disposition
127

About The Author
137

Acknowledgement

To my good family and friends, thank you for being uniquely you, each and every one of you.

TRUTH BEING BONDAGE: A Memoir. Copyright © 2021 by Mo Abbie. All rights reserved. No part of this book may be reproduced in any manner whatsoever without written permission except in the case of brief quotations embodied in critical articles and reviews. No part of this book may be stored in a retrieval system or transmitted in any form by any means. This includes electronic, mechanical, photocopying, recording or otherwise without prior written consent of the publisher.

Fortified One books may be purchased directly for educational, business, or sales promotional use. For information about bulk purchases, please contact Fortified One for special sales requests at sales@fortifiedone.com .

Printed in USA 1st Edition: July 2021. Published in the USA by Fortified One, website: www.fortifiedone.com. For further inquiries contact info@fortifiedone.com .

Manufactured or Printed in the United States of America
ISBN: 978-1-7367008-2-2
Library of Congress Control Number: 2021903595

First Printing, 2021

IS IT ME

Just let her down easy. That was the mindset of my exes. I had the least messiest breakups of anyone I knew. Since relocating to a mid-size city that sometimes poses as a small town, dating has been the pits. This is something I had never thought to consider. Dating back home in a major metropolitan was easy. If I wanted to meet someone new, no problem. It was just a matter of stepping outside for a few. The men back home were bold and straight forward. They knew what they wanted and went for it with no hesitation. I noticed there were a lot of married couples in this new town. Most of the couples seems to have married their high school sweethearts.

After talking to a friend in this new town she said that if a man isn't married by age 30, he isn't into women. That was harsh, since 30 is still fairly young. There is no guarantee that you will find the one by a certain age. In the big city men dated around because there were more options. I would not view a man as not being into women simply due to his age. People fall in and out of love all the time. It is comforting to know when you have found the real deal.

So, here I am at the time tumbling down into my 30's. Dare I reflect that, maybe I am the problem. Imagine that... a woman being open enough to take accountability for her actions or inactions. Looking back, just about all my relationships have ended on fairly good notes. I never had to endure any physical altercations in a relationship. Although, I did experience some lightweight emotional and mental abuse. It was nothing I could not handle or walk away from. I have an incredibly low tolerance for nonsense. Any type of abuse will not stand with me.

The funny thing is my relationships normally end in compliments and apologies. I've heard, "you deserve better" one too many times. And who am I to argue that. Some women sink their hooks in deeper at this point because they don't want to be alone. I will not force my love on to someone who is looking to turn away. After hearing this same tune one too many times, I will make the improvements necessary to obtain better.

Let's just say, in case I find myself standing across someone who wishes to share these words again. My new stance in that moment is to make an inquiry. Do you have someone else in mind that you feel is more suitable for me? Hook me up with that person, then you can leave. Not saying that I would hold someone in a relationship against their will. Just hook me up is all I'm saying.

The fact is there is, there is no way I would let someone try to hold me in a situation neither one of us desires to be in. If that person asked me to hook them up with someone, I feel that is fair. It would have to be someone I am not close too but fitting for them. If the person has serious character flaws, I will not match them with anyone and make sure they know why.

No matter how many times I have heard "you deserve better." It surprises me every time I hear it. If I am blessed beyond what I feel I deserve, I would thank God for my blessings. Go on, receive those blessings openly and happily. I love a man who is multi-layered in a positive way, that is what I go for. I look beyond what is seen on the surface or basic criteria that one would normally look for in a mate. Handyman attributes is a major one for me. That results in saving us money on possible home or auto repairs. Those who act on their personal growth challenges to obtain goals are wonderful. It shows that you are a person who does not just settle.

Women have been called out for dating a man's potential. Consider me guilty of this. It is not just about what you want him to see and manifest. He must see that same potential as a reality within himself.

I decided to take on a self-examination. The question I can't help but pose to myself, are these guys leaving something out when we break up? Am I being spared some painful truth to protect my feelings? The energy they give is as though they are standing in the way. Almost as if they were blocking the lane for my true mate to arrive. That could be the case.

Maybe, I am physically present but not there in the moment. This may be closer to the truth. Sometimes I feel as though I am running a race parallel to my life. I could have focused on the present when that is what matters most.

As for my character, I have been told that I am a good person on many occasions. My favorite compliment came from a male friend who told me that I was the most righteous person he knows. In the past, I have been known to be extremely quiet, shy at times. This dates back to my childhood years, some of those traits still show up from time to time. Others may describe me as a go-getter, outgoing and humorous. You would think that two different people are being described. I agree with all the above. I don't like being boxed in. I would never say I am just one thing. I try to be as fair and honest dealing as I can be at all times.

For some reason I never cared for a lot of attention. Sometimes I would go out of my way to divert attention from myself. I have always tended to tread very lightly. I would move about in a way mousy to stay out of the spotlight. For all I know, it maybe some form of undiagnosed social anxiety.

On the flip side, if I were more of a social butterfly, I am sure there would have been more connections to relish in. At minimum I would have increased my earning potential. Let me continue reflecting back.

THE HOME I REMEMBER

My childhood would be considered to be stable in many ways. At home, I had my parents and my brother Ben. He was four years older than me. As far as moving around goes, I only had two addresses up to the time I became an adult.

The place where I spent my tot years was a large one-bedroom apartment in a Courtyard style Yellowstone brick building in the Austin neighborhood of Chicago. Dad worked during the day, while my brother went to school. I would be home with my mother. She would teach me all the things necessary for my introduction the school and the world.

I had my daily dose of Sesame Street and Mr. Rogers, while Mom would later watch some soap operas. But her favorite form of entertainment wasn't the television, she loved music. She would play the radio all the time or some records from her massive record collection. There was an exposed top record player that sat on top of a heavy wood jukebox style record player console. I always thought the larger wood record player was just an accent décor piece, since it was never used.

There was an ivory-colored coffee table set in the living room. The base had a hollow carved paisley style decoration on it. Ben and I would stick things in there for fun like papers and wire hangers, especially wire hangers. The tabletops were glass with leopard prints. The side tables were octagon shaped. One of the side tables had a missing glass top. In its place Mom glued on copper pennies to cover the top. Every so often, we would have guests over who would come to pry the pennies from the table. The common reason was to get a snack from the store or to have a few cents for tax. I had occasions when I needed a few cents for tax and that table would be my source. For the most part, whatever was taken was replaced and glued back down when we had change.

The dining room had a dark walnut china cabinet with a matching dining room table and chairs. It seemed like a different wooden chair from the set would break every couple of years. Also, there was Ben's bed. It sat against the other wall in the corner passively noticeable. It was more dark walnut blending in with the room. The bed had a trundle underneath, which I've never seen anyone use. The top mattress would collapse with the slightest amount of weight applied. Two small kids sitting on top is all it would take for the mattress to cave in.

The kitchen was blah. I remember yellow and green, true 60's / 70's retro remaining. We played outside on the back. There was plenty of space all concreted in for our playing pleasure, I suppose. There was always a dreary look out back. It may have been due to the way the three-story buildings stood connected. The different staircases from each entryway all funneled out to the same concrete quad.

The only bedroom in the apartment was fairly large. It had a matching set of walnut color wooden bedroom furniture with ornamental details and dark oil-rubbed bronze handles. As the youngest, I shared the room with my parents. This is where we would congregate after dinner and watch popular television shows like The Jeffersons, The Incredible Hulk and Solid Gold.

I was once caught standing in my parent's bed mimicking the dance moves of Solid Gold dancers. It seemed funny to me how they would expose one shoulder and roll it around with fire in their eyes. One day it was just me and Ben in the room. He was sitting on the bed and here I go. I pulled out my little shoulder through my shirt collar and started rolling it around with my back to the door. And unbeknownst to me, Mom walks in and... WHOP! A swap to my backside. "What do you think you're doing, said Mom?" I was startled and hurt at the same time.

"I was just doing the dance that they are doing on tv," I explained.

"You don't do everything you see on tv. I bett' not ever catch you dancing like that again," she said!

I tried to reason, "But, I was just doing what they were doing."

"Do it again," she said swiftly! I dropped it, I was probably no more than 2 or 3 years old at the time. I didn't even know what it meant to be dared and I dare not find out!

Dad was something else too. Outside of the pictures we would take at family gatherings, Ben and I was the focus at home. There was one picture taking session that was hilarious to me. Dad had prepared to take a family photo. Mom and I sat in a chair while Dad called for Ben to stand next to the chair.

Ben comes to the front room. "Boy, get back there and go put some pants on," said Dad. Ben goes back to the bedroom. Time passed by, then Dad calls again for Ben to return. Ben comes back into the room and nothing has changed.

"Boy, why you ain't put no pants on, you cain't take no pictures with your drawls on. Standing up here in your drawls boy, what's wrong with you" Dad wondered out loud?

It was the most hilarious thing I had ever heard in my short life at the time. Retelling this story as a pre-teen, I thought I was around 5 years old. Then one day the picture resurfaced and I was a baby laying across my mother's lap in a blanket. I was shocked because I remember busting a gut at the time and getting the hiccups.

Dad had a voice inflection that was uncommon. His normal tone was as if he was irritated all the time, especially with us. So, we knew to keep things short with him. Around that time, I had no problems when Dad would go off like that. So long as, his issues stayed there with Ben. It was entertaining to me. But over time these little front street jabs and put downs took a toll on Ben's self-esteem.

Mom was the warmest yet toughest woman you could ever meet. She would not start trouble with anyone. But, if she found herself in conflict, she would finish it on top, man or woman. Her battles were so much so, that her siblings nicknamed her Hard Rock. I did not like that she was given such a rough nickname, but she took it lightly. It was just something amongst family to have a lighthearted laugh. Some of the stories that got back to me when I got a little older, it became obvious the name kind of fit.

Mom's side of the family would come around from time to time. Either one at a time or a group of aunts, uncles or cousins. At other times there would be a large family gathering to celebrate a holiday or birthday. We have the best times when we would all come together to celebrate.

One Christmas, we waited quite some time for family to stop by. Mom had cooked dinner. Next thing we know, the evening had turned into night. Mom figured no one was coming by. She stored away the food and we put on our pajamas to get ready for bed. As soon as we headed to the bedroom the doorbell rings. Mom's eldest two brothers came by first. A few minutes later the doorbell rings again and family after family pours through the door. Next thing we know, we have a full house.

That Christmas the family did not stay long. It was late. They just stopped by to show some love. A couple of folks grabbed some to go plates. And of course, a few pics were taken. Mom was captured in her house duster coat. No quick change was made. She was simply happy that everyone came together.

Both of my parents smoked cigarettes and drank liquor, mostly beer in my younger years. It was more of a social thing. As a young early riser, as if I had a job. I would watch Dad take a swig out of his flask that was embroidered with .38 pistol before work.

I was such an explorer. Not that I had far to go. I had to peep around new corners to see what was behind these walls.

Music played a major part in our lives. I came into the picture as music was making major transitions. There was a lot of funk, some disco, pop and soul R&B being played on the radio. Though Mom was a big blues fan. There was some gospel on the radio that had become popular in the mainstream as well. I loved the positivity.

A song I did not know the name of or the artist would cause me to cry every time I heard it. That song was Holding You, Loving You by Don Blackman. It was it was instantaneous after the first few cords. It was out of my control and I did not understand it. This song would have me crying on demand. Luckily, I was able to rediscover this song about 30 years later. Most likely, I gravitated to the beautiful instrumentation in the composition. At such a young age, I knew this composition was undeniably beautiful.

As music shifted from funk and disco, the synthesized sounds of the early 80's were broadened by the clarity of FM stations. Polished productions took over and left the 70's sound behind. I asked Mom if there were other songs that sounded like this (high quality and clear). I figured this music was hidden and wondered why we had not been listening before. At the time, I was too young to know about the progression of music.

One of the most polarizing changes to music was the advent of the rap music genre. I remember enjoying the song Good Times by Chic. Not too long thereafter there was a song called Rappers Delight by Sugar Hill Gang with the exact same beat.

TRUTH BEING BONDAGE

I liked both songs but preferred Chic because it came first and reminded me of when our family got together, good times.

The first rapper I remember was Curtis Blow. He threw off my short time reference for holiday season when the Christmas Song was released. I would always think it was gift getting time. But the song was so hot it played way into the summertime in the early days of rap music.

WE ROLL

Mom and I would ride the bus on rare occasions, even though Mom and Dad both had a car. Dad drove a tan mid-70's Oldsmobile Delta 88 that was very reliable. It took on a role as the family car. He always kept fresh forest pine air freshener in his car. Before there was a major push to wear seat belts in the mid to late 80's, no one I knew wore seat belts. Around that time, I would stand up for much of the duration of the ride. Not sure if it was a matter of me feeling like I wanted to be a part of whatever was going on in the front seats or to have a better view. Whatever the reason, I felt like I had to stand up and watch.

Every Sunday Dad would take Ben and I out to his sister, Aunt Rosie's house. I surfed the backseat standing as usual. I held on to the front seat headrests from one side of town to the other. It was around a 40-minute drive to Aunt Rosie's.

One Sunday, on a drive out to Aunt Rosie's, my legs got tired during the drive for the first time. I was conflicted about sticking to my tradition of standing the entire way. We had just hopped off the expressway and were about 5 minutes away. I finally sat down. It was such a relief and soothing. I sat there wondering, why I had not done this sooner.

But just as I sat down, we emerged from under a viaduct to approach the intersection. I looked up to my left and saw cars approaching the intersection. Then I looked up front and saw the light turn yellow as we were in the middle of the street crossing. For some reason, it felt like Dad was driving exceptionally slow. Looking straight ahead the entire time. Dad did not notice the cars approaching. He also seemed unaware of the traffic lights changing.

As we are heading east bound on 63rd street. Here comes a newer model wood grained panel station wagon straight into our direction. Then bam! This station wagon hits us right in the middle of the driver's side. The accident knocked me back on my feet then, slid me to the passenger side. Dad checks on us to see if we are okay. He then pulls the car over to the curb.

That newer station wagon was not so cute anymore. The whole front end was crunched up. Headlights were busted and the front bumper grille fell off. Dad got out of the car, talked to the guys and exchanged information. I remember him doing a lot of laughing. I thought this was a strange reaction for an accident. You just got t-boned, with your kids in the car.

After about 10 minutes, we were back in route to Aunt Rosie's. We get out of the car to see the damage. It was as if nothing had happened. No dents and no scratches. We could not help but laugh because that station wagon was destroyed. That dang car earned it's keep!

Mom's car on the other hand, was a beast all its own. It was an early 70's maroon Plymouth Fury. It got us from point A to B most of the time. I would say maybe a third of the time it hesitated to start. But Mom would keep working with it. She would work that crank shaft and pump that gas petal. All the while, being aware to not flood the engine until she got the right combo for a startup. I never saw Dad near this car. He may have moved it for her or taken it to the shop, but never just cruising around.

I could not stand that vehicle. The only good thing about the car was that it was huge. We would spend a lot of time with extended family. It was great in the sense that we could get two or three families in the same car together. Adults and children in most cases had their own seat, without having to sit on someone's lap.

The car had huge rust holes on the floorboard of the driver's and passenger's side. I would always relate this car to the Flintstones. Just being young and honest I would ask Mom if she was going to drive with her feet, like they did on the cartoon. The only thing keeping me from falling out of the car were heavy rubber floormats.

When we had extra passengers, most of the time I had to sit up front in the middle seat. The middle seat belt had been lodged between seat a long time ago. So as a precaution, I had to ride standing up holding the dashboard in case there was an accident. If you were not paying attention, oops, that was your forehead. Especially, if she had to hit the brakes hard. I had gotten so accustomed to riding in the car standing up, which is why I rode in Dad's backseat the same way.

The time that stood out most with this car. One hot summer day, we set out to go to the store. The car had dark colored vinyl seats that sat out in the blazing sun. I had on short pants that apparently had been shorter than usual. The scolding pain I felt from my legs grazing the smoldering seats was the worse. Until this day, I still avoid any shiny seating like leather. I know these materials are totally different. Leather is breathable and does not hold on to heat like vinyl. Someday I'll come around. I have given up the added value of leather for cloth seats.

I also learned early on about being left in hot cars. Mom would roll down or crack the windows while she would make runs. When there was no parking available, she was a notorious double parker. I used to think parking officers were our friends. They would come by to say hi and gave a little small talk. All the while leaving a parking citation for Mom on the windshield. Just goes to show that everything and everybody is not what it seems on the surface.

Independent vendors would sell items near the off ramp of the expressway. They had the best roasted peanuts. They also sold oranges, watermelons, pork rinds and skins. There would even be fresh fish you could purchase along the side of the road. The fish sellers said their catfish was Mississippi farm raised. It may have been a marketing hook for the many people who migrated from there.

On rare occasions my mother would give me a few swallows of her beer. She said that it helped to kill germs and worms. I did not like the taste of it, but I went along with it. After talking to some of my cousins, I found out their mothers would also have them take their occasional swig. I soon caught on that this was a forbidden adult only drink and that small swig we got was an exception.

One day at a big family gathering at my Aunt Mary's house. Mom cracked open an ice-cold Miller Highlife. She called me over to take a few swallows. I had made up my mind as soon as she called me over that I would try to drink up as much as I could. My little self, was a boney well-known picky eater. I just took the can and turned it up. This was mainly to have bragging rights amongst my cousins. I had given myself some sort of adult rite of passage. The time was right. Mom was fully engaged in a conversation and was not paying attention. I drank and drank and would not stop. Mom had to snatch the can from me.

"Girl, what do you think you're doing? This girl done damn near drunk up my whole beer. That's enough for you. No more beer for you, I see you don't know how to act," Mom stated furiously.

In my mind, it was mission accomplished. Especially since there was no whooping behind it. Apparently, she didn't blame me. I jetted outside to tell my cousins that I just drank a can of beer. They knew it was true because my mother was still complaining inside.

My plans to become a toddler drinker were dashed after that moment. She stopped giving us that swig of beer. Our new worm killer was an old southern go to. She gave us castor oil.

She said it would clean us out. That did not go far. I could not stand the smell, let alone taste it.

Aunt Mary's house was the place to be. She had five children all had either become adults by the time I came along, or they were just shy of adulthood. Her youngest, a girl, was close to Ben's age. You would get your fill of life there. Love, food, entertainment, games, music, you name it. There may have been elements like gambling, cussing and smoked filled rooms. All the taboos of adult life the children were curious of. This experience allowed us to peer into the future. Our curiosity was always culled. We could not sit around the adults.

The parental discretion was to, "go outside and play" or "go in the other room with the rest of the kids". That was fine, there were plenty of kids around the same age and everybody enjoyed each other's company. The boys would play softball while the girls would jump rope. When we played indoors, we would play Hide and Go Seek or Simeon Says. Pocket change would get you very far because the best penny candy stores were around there. Frozen icy cups, cookie bags, candy varieties like Now & Laters, Lemonheads, Jawbreakers, candy necklaces and big pin wheel lollypops could be purchased for just a few cents.

Mom had our day set aside for Aunt Mary's house as Saturday. She would go there on Friday's, but no kids allowed. Well, kids were allowed just not her kids. I did not understand at the time. Later, I understood. We could not be there due to things being taken up a level. We would hear some of the wildest stories from our cousins. According to many witnesses, I was told that Mom would beat and slap grown men. This is something Ben and I did not experience up close, but the rest of the family found it hilarious. She was a no-nonsense kind of woman. You will not beat her or get over on her family.

Gambling was their favorite form of entertainment. Card and dice games mostly took place at Aunt Mary's and Aunt Mattie's on occasion. As far as I could tell, my parents gambling never got out of hand to the point where there was a gambling problem. Due to the gambling, Aunt Mary's house became a target for robbers. Most likely sore losers looking to get their money back and then some. There were no attempts to break in while no one was home. One robbery involved some guys kicking in the door while the house was full of people. Taking all the cash on the table and taking from some individuals.

After one return home from Aunt Mary's. We went up the courtyard into our building, up to our front door. Instead of opening the door as usual, Mom had her keys out but just stood there with Ben and I. We looked up at her face and she was crying. I had never seen her cry before. She was the person who would get me to stop crying and on to something else. Even though we asked her what was wrong she never said what was on her mind. We had no clue as to what we could do to help. All I knew was something was not right. That day will remain a mystery. After spending a few minutes in the hallway looking at the front door, she slowly turned the key to let us in. We were relieved but as we entered the music was blaring loudly from the stereo. She heard it. I did not pay it much attention to it outside the door, as I was just ready to get in the house.

My guess at the time was that Mom thought something was going on in the home. She may have thought my Dad was entertaining another woman. Or someone was robbing the home but using the stereo as a distraction. Dad rarely used the stereo. He had a little transistor type radio where he would only listen to talk radio, sports or some gospel music on the AM channels. He only had one 45 rpm record compared to Mom's massive record collection of 45's and 33 1/3's. Maybe she left it on before we left. The only thing is that it was considerably louder than what we were used to. My best guess is that she gambled away some money that was not supposed to be used to play with. Perhaps it was the rent, utilities or someone else's money they were holding.

Before the gambling boat and local casinos came along, adults would go to the racetrack when they wanted to do something different. The kids could go on a few lucky occasions. Mom would pick up betting sheets from these small wooden shacks about the size of an outhouse and show me how to read the odds. You could end up with a few dollars from generous adults who would share their winnings with you when tagging along.

The lottery also was big in the family. My mom would mostly play her numbers straight but mostly box. Playing box increased the chances of winning if the numbers came in scrambled. She liked to dream her numbers. There were a couple of books she would use to look up numbers that matched up to dream scenario's that were depicted in the books. One day I randomly wrote a three-digit number on the wall. Instead of a spanking Mom played the numbers. The numbers came in and paid off for her right away. It was a lucky guess on my part. After that, she would ask if I had any numbers to add to her list of numbers. This only went on for a short time. The numbers were not paying off as quickly as they did that first time.

My parents met in Chicago both were from the deep south in neighboring states. From what I gather from Dad, they met at a lounge. He said himself a guardian angel, a supernatural woman told him, "you better go get her before you lose her" and Mom appeared in his path. Soon after that statement was made the angel disappeared. He credits her for their meeting. That was the only time I ever heard Dad speak of a supernatural experience. I got this story as a young adult and he spoke it with conviction.

They both left the south for better opportunities up north. Mom worked as a Book Binder periodically, but she was primarily a homemaker. Dad was a Steel Worker up until he retired due to health issues.

There were shows of opulence like Lifestyles of the Rich and Famous. If that show did not teach me anything else, it taught me we definitely were not rich. We also were not extremely poor. We never had a bone bare refrigerator. After seeing a bare fridge at a friend's home before all I could think was, how? I figured we were somewhere in the middle. I asked Mom if we were middle-class. She said we were not even that. Where do we fit? She said we were lower to moderate class. I accepted moderate class. Poor and low just sounded so hopeless. Give us a fighting chance, at least.

We were bargain shoppers. We shopped at several vibrant retail strips along Madison and Pulaski on the Westside especially the Three Sisters chain. We also frequented a shopping strip in Chicago formerly known as Jewtown on Roosevelt and Halsted. Today it is referred to as Maxwell Street. One occasion we had to take a parking space a bit further off the strip due to movie scenes being filmed. I was later told that movie was Blues Brothers.

Maxwell Street also had the best polish sausages ever. This became my first favorite food after Mom introduced them to me. Competition came a few years later when I had my first Italian Beef almost any hole in the wall restaurant would do. Rib tips from a joint called Freddine's that once existed on the Westside, was a big hit. The french fries hidden underneath the bread and ribs benefited from the bbq sauce and grease trickling down to the bottom of the basket. Then there is a Chicago favorite, mild sauce. The mild sauce was a peculiar orange sauce I first tried on the south side slathered on top of a bag of plain potato chips. It is a fried chicken topping staple at places like Uncle Remus and Harold's Chicken Restaurants.

We would take trips down south, but this became less frequent as time moved along. On one trip Mom, Ben and I all crammed into my cousin Dena's little grey sports car along with her son and daughter. Both were around our ages. It was a long ride being lodged somewhere against the arm rest for about 12 hours. We arrived sometime in the wee hours of the morning. We sat down on a couch. The adults talked amongst each other.

A young man comes in to offer me an apple. I was fine, not hungry just a kind of tired. I said no. "Take the apple," Mom said. "I don't want it," I replied. We went back and forth about this apple nobody wanted. Then next thing I know she unleashes several smacks to my backside. She had some swift hard hands, there was truly no difference in whether she would whoop you with a belt, a switch or her hands. She was not the type of mother who would look for belts or keep throwing out threats about finding a switch. If that butt whooping was immediately warranted, those hands were ready now!

This is the whooping that took place in my early years I would never forget. It was not necessarily the pain. It was more so, for what? My sense and logic kicked in early I would say. All this just for saying no. Maybe it was a southern thing. Was I not mannerly enough? Should I have said no, thank you? Perhaps I was supposed to take everything from anyone who has something to offer me. Maybe she was hungry.

So, after being forced to take this dang apple and say thank you, I still handed it off to her. She could have told the young man in the first place I'll take it and hold on to it for later. I am sure he was related and just making a nice gesture. I was not familiar with him. The whole situation made no sense to me then and to this day I do not comprehend the lesson in all of this.

Outside of the rambunctious gatherings, my parents were eternally peaceful. Their favorite pastime was fishing. It was a major contrast to city life. We just about never fished in the city. There was a public lagoon only some feet away from our back door and we were less than 10 miles from Lake Michigan. We would go to towns north or far west of the city like McHenry and Aurora, IL. Mom would get us up at insanely early times. It would still be dark out while packing up food, snacks and bait. While arriving at our destination, the sky would start to brighten after driving about an hour. The ploy was to get the best fishing spots. I only recall one or two outings where we barely caught anything. Most fishing trips were highly successful.

Our most frequent recreation place was McHenry Dam. Which was my favorite. Evergreen trees were at the opening of the park. There was a large wooden deck fishing pier that lead out onto the river. My favorite parts of the park were the playground, concession stand and the dam waterfall.

Mom and Dad had fishing reels, they would set out two or three each. Ben and I had fishing poles. As Ben got a little older, he was able to have a fishing reel. Dad would venture out from our designated fishing area. He would look for spots where the larger fish were biting. He mostly caught channel catfish, silver bass, big mouth bass and buffalo carp. He would use minnows to catch fish. It seemed over time the fish started to evolve. It was as if they were no longer interested in worms and minnows.

By Mom and I being closer to shore we mostly caught perch, bluegill sunfish and bass. I did not mind the worms that we fished with. It was the occasional prick from the hook that got me.

There were times when Dad would catch frogs or turtles. He would turn those special catches over to my uncle and cousin on Mom's side of the family.

There was no catch and release going on with us. It was more like catch and eat. We would bring a cooler full of fish home. Mom, Ben and I would clean the fish with scales with dull knives. Dad would skin the catfish with his pliers then gut all the fish. After all the fish were cleaned and prepped Mom would season and bread the fish and cook them that evening. Any surplus fish she would freeze for future dinners or give to other family members.

Fishing trips played out best when we had guests come with us. A common pairing was my aunt on Mom's side. Aunt Felicia we called her Aunt Lee, along with her husband Uncle Roy. They had three kids two boys who were a little closer to

Ben in age and a girl who was just a couple of years younger than me. We would play on the swings, sliding board, seesaw and merry-go-round. It was a goodtime for all.

Aunt Lee had some of the nicest things. She was such an inspiration growing up. She had a lovely long plush Brougham Cadillac. As she paid her highway tolls sometimes the toll arm would come down too fast on the trunk of her car due to its length.

I was left behind for one of the fishing trips. I was particularly upset because Aunt Lee's family was meeting up with my parents. They had planned to go to a fishing hole they rarely ventured to. The place was suspected to have snakes onsite. I told them I was not scared. Cousin Roslyn was going, and she was younger than me. My pleas were ignored. They went out of the way to make a trip to the southside housing projects. Where my cousin & Aunt Emma would babysit me. Emma was my Dad's niece who married Mom's brother, Uncle Les.

Once I learned the order of the day. I had to deal with not going. I was totally done. This is the first time I recall ever visiting their home and I was hysterical. We got on the elevator and it reeked of piss. I was so done! I gave them absolute terror! I cried and cried, screamed and screamed. To calm me down Emma's son Terry got his graduation cap and gown. He had me put it on and it overflowed my little frame. He had me stand on a chair. I did so uncooperatively. Then he started taking pictures. He did a good job of distracting me by saying a bunch of positive things and doing a full-on photo shoot. He changed up the limited wardrobe and had me trying different poses. It wasn't so bad after I got comfortable.

Some weeks later, they gave my parents the photos after the film was developed. Anyone could tell I was terribly angry at the start of the photos.

As we got older, the coordination of fishing trips was not as well thought out as it could have been. We would meet Aunt Lee's family on some Sundays. This was her only true day off that was convenient for her family to meet us. The problem was these were the days of the Bulls playoff run against the Pistons. These trips should have been cancelled altogether. We did not have cable or a VCR so we would hurry back home to catch the 3rd or at least the 4th quarter of the game on TV.

Around this time, I developed some type of motion sickness. It seemed to be related to the movement of water and the sun's reflection off the water. I would be in bad shape and very nauseous by the time we made it home. The perfect remedy for me was a chocolate malt from one of the neighborhood stores. I was back to myself and no more nausea after consuming the malt. It cost about 70 cents. It was so delicious and lucky for me it was my cure.

CHAPTER 4

LIFTING THE VEIL

We experience life in real time. Adults, especially parents are tasked with passing along wisdom and guiding the youth in the right direction. Should they stray off that path, we count on our elders to guide them back to their righteous center.

In our early years, our first lessons are learning our basic senses, surroundings, language and the alphabet. The next big lesson is learning the difference between good, bad and evil. Lessons are picked up quickly when a child receives praise for all the good things they do. Children are applauded for reaching learning milestones. It is amazing to watch a child grow in their learning capabilities.

Whenever a child acts outside of what we consider to be good characteristics, they know it. We normally label it as bad behavior. Children pickup on negative reactions to their actions. This correction of bad behavior helps to keep them centered and grounded. It also lays the groundwork for learning acceptable behavior.

As for evil... where to start? Hopefully, a person's intuition and instinctive nature will alert them of evil. Especially, when they have not been briefed or studied on the immediate presence of such a thing in their surroundings. Evil is the worst. It is ill willed and ill intentioned.

Mom first alerted me on who a bad or evil person was. This character was mashed up in a story relating to stranger danger. The stranger was none other than the Boogeyman. Mom and Ben made him sound so horrid I could not even put a face to him. The stories sometimes sounded so farfetched that I had trouble believing them. Ben co-signed the story, this made things more believable for me.

I was told that sometimes the Boogeyman may have candy. So, if someone I did not know offers me candy, as much as I loved candy. Say no thank you and leave. Do not go to that person or get close. Do not get in a stranger's car, even if they claim to know my parents.

I still wanted a visual of the legendary Boogeyman's face from a magazine, newspaper or something. This way I could know when to go in the other direction.

One spring day, Mom and I took a walk down to a local currency exchange. While we were waiting at the cross walk to cross a main road a girl who was about my age was standing at the adjacent cross walk with a lady who most likely was her mother. Until then, all my encounters with young people my age were positive. They would say hi, smile or want to play. This little girl's spirit was already tainted. She looked in my direction, stuck out her tongue and put up her middle finger. Mom did not see her. And I wish I didn't see her. I asked Mom, what did all that mean? Mom broke it all down for me. It was bad enough that I did not know this little girl, but what's eating you already as a toddler?

When we get into the currency exchange, I stood there with my hand in Mom's coat pocket. I do not remember moving around at all. Something felt off. Mom wore a tan trench coat and black dress shoes. Someone else had on the same tan trench coat with black dress shoes. Looking up at the back of their heads both people looked similar. I then went over to the other person and put my hand in their pocket. I was not reprimanded for wandering off. For the longest time, I thought that I had been swapped out to another family. I asked Mom about it a couple of times. She had a simple answer for my inquiry which was, "cut it out!" That was the demeanor of the Mom I remember. Plus, my surroundings appeared to be the same.

The first encounter I had with deception and mischief was on behalf of Ben. Mom snapped a picture of it. From the looks of the picture, I was not walking at the time. I was placed at the rear of the sofa set chair, likely to support my back. I was in a dark colored dress and barefoot. I really didn't need the picture to remember the moment. It was just surprising to go back and see how small I was at the time because I remember many of these events vividly.

As I sat there minding my own baby business, Ben pops up. Okay Ben, what's happening? He then reaches behind his back and puts this awful mask over his face. I screamed hysterically, as a baby would. He then took it off. Ben said, "it's not real, see look!" He dangled it in front of me and had me touch it. He put it on again, I still screamed. Hell, it's still ugly. He repeated the act of putting the mask on and off a few times so that I could get over my fear.

About a year or so later, I was able to go trick or treating with Ben. We did not leave our building. We stuck to the apartments that were in our entry way. This limited our score to only five other apartments. No complaints from me. My first time out to a candy giveaway. One or two apartments did not answer their doors. In all we did alright with what we had to work with.

Once we made it back down to our place on the first floor, Mom immediately grabbed our pumpkin headed candy baskets. "I need to check the candy to see if it was tampered with. There are some sick people out here in this world," Mom said.

Mom broke apart or mashed up the candy. The candy looked terrible. I told her I didn't want it anymore. The fancy wrappers and smooth surfaces of the candy is what I thought it was all about. All this mashing and smashing would surely take away the flavor. A tear or two may have been shed over my precious sweets.

"I want to make sure there are no sharp objects or anything that can harm you in it," Mom said. What in the world? That was my thought at the time, I had not learned the F word yet. Mom tried a bit of the candy to reassure me that it had passed her goodness inspection. I went ahead and tried some with her. She was right. Same great taste. After that reveal I was over trick or treating. Perhaps we should not take any candy from people we don't know. I will just eat what we have at home or what I can buy on my own from the corner store.

A couple of years later I started my first year of school. Here we go. Halloween rolls around again. The teacher and her assistant tell the class that they have a special treat for us.

After lunch, we take our normal bathroom breaks. As we walk down the hallway, we make a stop. Our teacher says we are about to go into a haunted house. I was not familiar.

As we move forward, the front of the class proceeds to descend a few stairs. I was down toward the end of the line. A girl who was about the third from the last in line screamed and panicked. I was right behind her. Before I could see what was wrong, I went on alert. She jumped out of line and headed in the opposite direction. Once I saw what was going on, I turned around to hit the exit as well.

We were both screaming and crying. When we went to run up the stairs, there were older students there blocking the way. They redirected us and made us go through the haunted house. This took place in the school's basement. We were weaving in and out of several rooms.

These haunted house terror providers were the older children at the school. The school went up to the 8th grade. They had props and dressed up in masks, makeup and homemade tattered Halloween garb. In every room, someone jumps out with their own look and terror act. The basement was dark with colored light bulbs. More and more screams lay ahead. Then finally, there was light ahead. We finally make it out of that place. Whose bright idea was it to have Kindergarteners go through a haunted house setting?

Mom would talk to me often about good and evil contrasts. Some people may seem good on the surface, but they may carry evil intentions. Over the years she would occasionally talk about an experience she had when she encountered JWG who harmed young boys and became well known after the discovery of his deeds. She spoke on how he came to the apartment building dressed as a clown when Ben was younger. She was happy at the fact that she could protect her son and that she had not fallen for anything he was selling.

Early on, Mom instilled an awareness of the society we live in. She would often say, "ain't nobody, no better than you!" She made sure we learned and knew this. The lady did not play. Even though she was born and raised in the deep south, she never bowed her stance. Mom reinforced the fact that, some things may not be real at times regardless of how it appears. Black or white, man or woman, rich or poor, it does not matter. No matter what they say or do or try to make you believe, always remember, "ain't nobody, no better than you!"

The lessons in jealousy came years later. For the longest time, I had equated jealousy with possessions. Someone having something bigger, or more of something another person does not have. As in keeping up with the Jones'. They have a larger house, more expensive cars or a greener lawn. These folks revolve their goals around trying to match or exceed what the Jones' have out of sheer jealousy.

The elements of jealousy will be learned, keep living. Unfortunately, you will encounter it. An odd but common practice for people to express their actions in a form of hatred. Which in most cases, is nothing more than jealousy. A person can express anger toward you because your hair is a couple of inches longer, your nails don't break as easily or you have both parents in your home. Minor things that fall in the normal order of your life can really set someone off if they have desired those things in their life. Regardless of how small you feel that detail of your life is. Save yourself some grief and avoid people who are jealous of you just for being you.

The first contrast in featurism I saw as a child was depicted on television. Images on TV in those days would show a separation between black and white. This separation between wealth and struggle was overtly attached to skin color. Good Times TV show featured a black family residing in Chicago housing projects. Over the course of the series there were a bunch of hard luck stories. None of these shows had white characters lived in housing projects. Most of the white shows depicted middle class families or luxurious opulence.

The only time black TV show characters were shown with better accommodations were if they are white adjacent. The Jeffersons for example, moved on up to a deluxe apartment with overwhelming majority white neighbors. Mr. George Jefferson was an anomaly to his neighbors and just about every person of his hue was just coming to visit.

There were also shows that would show black children given better accommodations by way of adoption. This was seen on shows like Different Strokes and Webster. The storylines showed black boys being in a circumstance to be adopted by rich white families. Not only did these shows make these young boys stars, but they were also incredibly cute. It is possible they may have been chosen for their roles due to their unique size. The star of Different Strokes, Gary Coleman, had a medical condition that limited his height, which kept him at a childlike size into adulthood. Emmanuel Lewis the star of the tv show Webster had no known medical condition but his height was also limited. He was 12 years old when the show premiered. The character he played on the show was 5 years old.

Some people may view these shows as simply entertainment. But there are plenty of coded messages in the concept and imagery of the shows alone. The older you get you see that much of this is done by design in the name of entertainment. It is truly the land of make believe.

One of the more unique lessons came to me in my toddler years. I would say it was particularly important in shaping how I think. To this day, I do not know who gave me this lesson. It was a young male. He showed me a dollar. It was the first time I had paid attention to one. Throughout my life, I thought everyone had received this lesson.

As I stood around the coffee table, the young man unfolded a $1 dollar bill. He showed me both sides of the US currency. He gave me a breakdown of the images displayed on the bill and his interpretations of symbolism. I was intrigued by the lesson. I had no understanding about money at the time. I just knew the obvious of having money to get the things we needed to keep up or enhance our standard of living.

I found it interesting that so much had gone into creating this currency. The part that stood out most was the all-seeing eye on top of the pyramid. At that time, I literally looked over my shoulder. As I looked on, I felt the presence of a veil. I knew at that moment; something was being hidden or something more was going on in the world that the average person was not privy to. When it comes down to the good, bad or extreme, I can't say that I am surprised by much.

A CRACK IN THE FOUNDATION

Since Mom's side of the family primarily resided on the Westside of town, naturally they visited the most. I cannot recall a time when Dad's family members would come around. Most of his family took to the Southside. We would see his family on the weekend when we visited Aunt Rosie.

The men on Mom's side of the family were close, good guys for the most part. They would freely give the kids change, a dollar or candy if they had it. Uncle Joe was known to come up with lightweight jobs or challenges to have the kids earn money for their work. Sometimes he would ask a kid for a cold glass of water. Simply fixing him a glass of water could earn you some quick candy store money. His payout would vary by age. The older you were, he would add a quarter or a dollar based on the task.

One day Uncle Joe asked the kids to wash his car. All the kids pitched in by taking different sections. Some focused on the interior, some did the exterior and scrubbed the white walls of his tires. After all the kids got his car nice and shiny, it was time to get paid. All the kids lined up. The teens got a dollar or two. The pre-teens got half-dollar coins. The younger kids got quarters. As he passed out the money, the coins started to run short. Some had to settle for broken change that added up to .25cents.

The little kids were not to be taken lightly. Ricky was cousin Janis' son, we were the same age. He was so furious with his great Uncle Joe for running out of change by the time he got to him. "I'm sorry Ricky, but I don't have any more quarters," Uncle Joe told Ricky. That set Ricky went off into trying to fight Uncle Joe. He was a tough tot and made his business known that he would not play about his money.

We were happy kids. The lesson in responsibility of earning our money was well received. It was more of a family oriented giving time. Washing the car was fun, the kids took on a role and owned it. Having a good time with water play doesn't hurt either. The jobs were welcome in case we got bored. Although, he probably should not have trusted some of the mischievous boys to bring his glass of water.

Mom was so special to me. Not only was she my mom and first teacher, but she was also my best and only friend in my early years. I would tell her everything. Ben was only 4 years older than me, but Mom was my go-to person. Dad was Dad, he was a nice guy. Although, his presence was intimidating. He would be gone most of the day working but home did not feel complete without him being there.

I finally got my own twin size bed. It was placed in my parents' room. I remember Mom combing my hair up towards the top of my head. As my hair stood straight up, she said, "that's a lot of hair for a 3 year old." She even snapped a picture. My bedframe was off white with a small flower vine design. I wore a pink vest holding my brown teddy bear who could not seem to keep his eyeballs attached to his furry face.

Around this time, I not only learned new words and their meanings. I started to learn about the world in general. There were also some words coming out of my mouth that should not have for someone my age. These occurrences would have put any adult on high alert. Clue number 1, someone was in my presence that had no business being around a child, had taken advantage of me.

These strange interactions seemed to take place in our bedroom at home. I cannot say with certainty if it was one young male or more than one with the same agenda. It was always a one-on-one interaction, no one else would be present in the room. This guy reached down my pants and asked, "if I liked it." Like what? How the hell would I know? Why are you getting sexual with a toddler? Lame ass!

I remember hearing the phrase, "keep a secret" a lot around those times. This person told me to keep this a secret. He threatened to kill my mom and my whole family if I told. Was I scared or afraid? No, I was not. For one, I was so young I did not even know what a secret was. I did not know what it meant to kill someone. What the hell are you doing to warrant such threats?

I would have my curiosity talks with Mom at night right before bed. Early night, it would just be the two of us. I'm sure I told her about a young male reaching in my pants and asking me if I liked it. I asked her what is a secret and what does kill mean? To this day I cannot stand for people to whisper in my ear.

One day, I go into a room. It looked just like our bedroom. There was a male sitting on the other side of the bed with his bare back turned. He throws a towel and tells me to put it over my face. When he threw the towel it partially covered my face. Then he came over to adjust it. I had no idea what was happening. I thought I was supposed to take instruction from adults or teens in charge.

Next thing I know, I am laying in the bed. From there, things went out of control. This person was on top of me. He kept fighting and tugging to keep my face covered. There was this constant, horrid, grating feeling. I hated the feeling. I could not get this person off me. The experience was very rough. My head was being slammed against the wall while all of this was going on. This person choked me. He then tried to smother me with a pillow. He pressed down with force. I was fighting for the entire time I stepped into that bedroom. Not sure if his goal was to silence my fighting and screams or to silence me forever. I had no idea what was going on. I certainly knew, this did not feel right and to put up a fight for my life.

I believe my oxygen may have been cut off at several points in this fight. I could not breathe when he attempted to smother me. I mean, he pressed this pillow down so hard. The only thing that saved me was my attempt to get air. With what strength I had left, I was able to turn my head to the side. That was the lifesaving move.

I am not sure if I passed out, but I definitely blanked out. This asshole continued jumping up and down on me while I struggled for my life. I questioned to myself, is this life? Is this what my days would be like from now on? It felt so terrible and never ending.

After it was all over, there was finally calm and silence. I came to the realization that it had finally stopped. I felt weary. I was still laying in the bed. The last thing I remember was looking at the furniture. It looked like our bedroom except things looked a little different. The furniture was still a dark walnut color but the handles on the drawers were a bright gold color. Our bedroom handles were darker, more of an antique oil rubbed bronze or brass.

I never captured the face of the person who committed this crime and I did not know many names back then. I do remember my mother kicking a young man out of our house one day. He exited out of the backdoor, while my mother yelled, "Don't Bring Your Ass Back Around Here No Mo!" This was the first time I had seen her totally irate.

The only other visitors I recall to our house were Dad's sons that he claimed from a previous marriage. His ex-wife had six children. According to him, she had three kids when he met her. He later told me that he married her to try and help her. She had come up from the south and had gotten entangled in some faction with a man of leisure. Of the six kids only the fourth child, Don was his.

Mom always referred to these young men who were teenagers at the time as my stepbrothers. I was only aware of the youngest three boys at the time. I didn't know about the total six children until I was much older. There was special emphasis on his son, Don. He would come to visit the house on his own at times.

The first time I paid attention to my stepbrothers coming around, we were home with Dad. He explicitly had Ben and I sit on one couch. He told the three young men to sit on the sofa across from us. He said no one could move from their seats. A few minutes of silence passed. These young men were staring us down. Don gets up from his seat to proceed over to Mom's record player. He picks up Mom's new Michael Jackson, Thriller album. It was her favorite album at the time. He turned on the record player, pulled the record out of the sleeve and placed it on the deck. After the needle dropped, he then starts doing this new technique with the record called scratching. We learn something new in these early days of hip hop, but in the process he ended up scratching Mom's favorite record. When he saw that he had damaged Mom's record, he got his two younger brothers and left.

Mom came home shortly thereafter. Ben jumped up with excitement and told her, "Don came over here." Mom turned to Dad and said in a firm tone, "I thought I told you... I didn't want him over here anymore."

"I had them on this couch, Ben and Mo were on the other. I didn't let them go anywhere," Dad said. Unbeknownst to Ben, he added fuel to the fire by telling her that Don just scratched her favorite record.

When I would tell Mom about these things about these strange encounters, at least I believe that she listened. When these topics came up, she would listen but rarely respond. She never showed a visible reaction to what I was telling her. She was good at answering most of my questions, especially when I sought out the meaning behind something.

After that horrible experience, occasionally I would ask: "Remember when that man... What was that?" "What happened to me?" "Why did he do that?" She never answered me when it came to that experience. Any other life lesson, she would readily answer my questions.

That horrific experience had caused me to become skeptic of young men. Especially, those in their teens and young adult men. This made me much more aware of my surroundings and more distrustful of people in general. My first challenge was a family gathering at our house. A young adult male cousin was standing in the pantry. He motioned for me to come into the pantry. I hesitated, even though he was the candy man. Luckily, it was a clean transaction.

"Why were you scared to come to me," he asked? I just said, "I don't know" to leave it alone. It was weird that he was standing in the pantry. He was not cooking or looking for anything, so why was he there? The lure of candy into a pantry was also a strange gesture.

Who can I trust? Well, at least I could at least depend on older men to do the right things. They always seemed wiser and more authoritative. The men on the verge of gray 40 years of age and older. At least, so I thought.

The interaction that occurred after the most horrendous experience of my life pretty much took the cake and ruined my trust for all men. I am not 100% sure of who committed the violation. All I have is my recollection and I later drew my own conclusions. I leave no man exempt in my case review of possible suspects, regardless of relationship.

The only other older adult male that came around a little more often than the rest of the family was Uncle Les. He was cool and liked to play when others did not want to be bothered. He was someone I trusted. I would ask Mom about him when he was not around. The other older adult male lived with me. This is the worst-case scenario. I am ready to face facts, not to save face for anyone.

Going about my day, I was alone in the living room of our apartment with an older man. He was in a chair drinking a beer. He called me over with a grin on his face. Unfortunately, this big devilish grin is all that I remember of his face. He unzipped his pants and pulled out his member. He then told me to kiss it. I said, "No! That's nasty, don't you use that to pee-pee?"

"It's not nasty it's good. It's like a lollypop," said the deceitful old man.

Although I cannot remember his face, I recall exactly what I was thinking. As these gestures were being made these are my exact thoughts at the time: 'Why you? Nobody has ever asked me no shit like this. (I was intrigued by cuss words at this age) This could have been anybody but you. I can't believe YOU are trying this with me, Not You!' I was so deeply disappointed in this person. My heart was so broken in that moment.

That night, while it was just Mom and I in the bed. I asked, "is a penis and a knuckle the same thing?" The wrinkles and crevices resembled knuckles to me. I'm sure at the time, I told her who it was that showed me and told me about a penis. I told her about this person urging me to kiss it by comparing it to a lollypop. I remember Mom correcting me on body parts. "No, those two things were not the same," she said. Besides answering my questions, I remember her being quiet. Maybe she was thinking.

Mom urged me to go to sleep. She left the bed once she thought that I had fell asleep. While I was alone in the bed, I started to go into a slight panic. I sat straight up in the bed. As much coaxing as that man tried to do, I knew it was wrong. It felt wrong, it just did not seem right.

The panicking started to increase. I repeated this man's relationship to me. The more I repeated, the more wrong it sounded. I started thinking, what if someone asks me about incident? How would I answer any questions about this violation? I can't say what made me panic about someone questioning me about this and finding out.

After all this panicking, I was a tired, exhausted toddler who just wanted to sleep so bad. But this horrid act had me wired up. In an apparent act of mental gymnastics, I came up with a solution. I prosed to self, if anyone asks about the incident, I will just say it was someone who you would not believe. That sounded perfect to me. That way I would not have to go through the pain of reliving the incident. The disappointment in that person nor would the relationship be relayed. Right there, I blew that experience up in my mind. Total deletion. No more!

I told the person I needed to tell, my mother. I purposely buried this problem to get some sleep. I intentionally got rid of this problem to stop the stress. I forgave myself of the shame that night, in order for me to live my life. I was a toddler. I had no idea what this effort of peace meant to me. I desperately needed peace. Especially since this person would be around me in some form. God gave me the peace of forgiveness before

I even knew what it was. If it is one of the two people, I believe it was that relationship is tarnished.

Mom did not reveal her emotions in front of me. I just hope that she handled this heartbreaking information accordingly. It was the first and last time an older man violated my space.

It seemed like I did not see much of Uncle Les after that. Even the family gatherings at our home seemed to slow down in the coming years. Once or twice a year would be it for us.

Around this time Dad changed. He became noticeably short tempered, fussy and angry when it came to me. Considering his ways with Ben, I probably should have saw it coming. I thought that attitude was solely reserved for his dealings with Ben.

A dramatic scene took place the next time I went to sit on Dad's lap. I did not see the difference from any other time I felt like doing so. "Get down, you cannot sit on his lap anymore. You are too old for that now," she said. It was strange because it was so abrupt. Next thing I know, Ben joins in. Ben came to pull me off Dad's lap. I cried and did not understand why this was happening. I had not even started elementary school yet.

Soon thereafter one day Dad came home from work. He bumped into my new big wheel. He went ballistic. "Get this damn thing out of the way," Dad yelled! I was horrified and hysterical. I was so scared. I had never seen this side of him. Mom got on him for yelling at me like that. I just curled up and cried my eyes out. I was not going to get anything. I couldn't, I was too heartbroken. I was not going anywhere near him.

Since that day he became fussy and easily irritated. This marks the time where a great distance grew between us. This was a fracture that was never repaired.

MO ABBIE

CHAPTER 6

HER REASONING, HIS STRESS

My impression after experiencing some strange encounters was, is this going to happen again. That was my biggest worry. I knew it wasn't right. It was a 3' ft fall. The reason I call it a 3' ft fall is because I was around 3 years old. The average height of a 3 year old is 3'ft tall. All that I could do was, go on.

One day, Mom and I had the strangest of nonverbal interactions. She was verbal by speaking with someone on the phone. It was most likely one of her sisters or one of the two cousins that she dealt with closely. We locked eyes in the mirror as I was walking past the bedroom. She said, "hopefully she is young enough to forget it."

I was so curious and inquisitive around this time. I could not help but wonder, who is she talking about? I was so sure she was not talking about me. I could not wait to find out which cousin she was referring to. At that stage, I started implementing the manners and etiquette I learned to allow her to finish her conversation. I normally would have interrupted right then and there. It was a kid that she was referencing by her saying the words, "young enough." My curiosity wanted to know what happened that was so bad that this kid should forget it? Will I one day lose my childhood memories, I wondered to myself?

I could see it in her eyes. She did not want to explain what or who she was talking about. I was proud of myself for being able to show a bit of growth and maturity by not asking questions. Something told me to spare her, let her live.

It is naïve to think that a person can do whatever to a child and they will just forget. Some people rehash trauma often, while others may push trauma to the farthest recesses of their mind. So far in fact that, they no longer think about it and forget that it happened. But that trauma makes a permanent imprint on their spirit. That negative energy has been released and it lingers. It shows up as fear and anxiety. Although that person may be unknowing of the source of fear.

That unnecessary physical trauma I endured ended up causing a urinary tract infection. I remember having a strong urge to urinate. As strong as that urge was, I could not go. Nothing would come out.

When I got older, Mom would warn me of the medicines I was allergic to. She told me that I was allergic to aspirin and penicillin. It was interesting because I could not recall when those medicines were ever prescribed. Putting the pieces together, it is my belief that the prescription was to help fight off the urinary tract infection at the least.

Around this time, Dad stopped smoking and drinking. It was the first time I had ever heard of the term, 'cold turkey.' There never any talk about what he was going to do or plan to do. The smoking and drinking was over for him. I didn't know what it meant or how things would be from here on out. All the adults I knew pretty much smoke and drank. I didn't know how he would fit with the others and their social habits. Being so young at the time, I had no idea 'cold turkey' was a rare feat. I thought going 'cold turkey' was how everyone broke their habits. I thought it was cool.

He was true to it. I never saw him smoke another cigarette. I saw him take his "last" drink. "Down the hatch," Dad called. And that was it. He never drank again on a regular basis. Although he would take a drink when a loved one passed away or once a rare holiday. Even then it would only be one drink and never overdone.

Ben and I were told that Dad's change in lifestyle was due to health issues. His primary issue was high blood pressure. This may have been the case, but the timing is suspect.

Dad took advantage of his job's medical benefits. He ended up in and out of the hospital over the next several years due to what they referred to as slight heart attacks. Things got scary a few times when he was admitted to the ICU. The scariest moment was a heart attack that resulted in a quadruple bypass surgery. He later said that bypass surgery was the worst thing he had experienced. The worst part was having his rib cage cracked open.

Whenever one of my parents were not in the home. Everything felt incomplete. I didn't feel whole and felt like something was missing. That was a scary time for us. Dad would be gone for weeks sometimes. We would visit him in the hospital. That is something I never grew accustomed to.

Was he really in such bad health or was it stress? He was over ten years older than Mom. He was 45 by the time they had me. So yes, he was becoming an older man but experiencing these things in his early 50's seemed kind of extreme.

After going through that ordeal, I wondered what they were both thinking. Did she ever talk to him about what happened to me? What was their discussion and what was their conclusions? If they did talk about it, what did they feel? Did Dad see me differently? Did he try to handle the person who violated me? Did he know more?

I would like to think that this was preventable. Obviously, we cannot change the past, but how do you rationalize this?

Looking at the bigger picture, Mom was a homemaker. She was totally dependent on my Dad for financial support. Starting over would have been a major undertaking. Any police involvement could have brought in social service investigations and ignited custodial issues. Was she trying to preserve relationships? Was she trying to save her marriage?

I still don't know what type of talk, negotiation or compromise that was made between the two, if any. I do know there was a game played. A game of pretend. Just sweep it under the rug. Children may forget a good amount of their childhood. Their way of handling the situation for me was, let's just hope that forgetfulness sets in and pray for the best.

LIFE SPLIT

This time marks our move from apartment living. My parents purchased a two-flat Greystone building also commonly known as a duplex in some areas. This move came in November a few months after my 5th birthday. The building was purchased months earlier. The occupants on the first and second level were given notice to move. The previous owner stayed around and paid rent, stating that he needed more time. As time dragged on, eventually the former owner had to be threatened with court action. The former landlord finally moved out. This helped to put our move in motion.

We moved into the first-floor unit. Lucky for us we had more family coming. My Aunt Candace or Candi as she was known, moved in with her fiancée and all but one of her children. Her eldest son who was in his late teens, decided to go his own way.

At the time, I did not know that Aunt Candi and her family were going to be our upstairs neighbors. Of course, there was more to the story than a child would need to figure out. I was surprised by the news because they were living in nice suburban townhouse. Plenty of yard space with play areas. They also lived across from cousin Janis. Her place had a similar set up.

Janis moved from the big city first to a town about 50 minutes away with her husband and kids. They both had five kids. Each kid in her family matched in age with Aunt Candi's kids. They definitely had a ball out there. We had fun as well when we would visit. Even though we only got to visit maybe twice. Mom did not trust her car at the time to get us there and back with no problems.

When we got to the new place, our bedrooms were already designated. All the bedrooms lined straight down one side of the house. Although none of the bedrooms were large, Ben ended up with the smallest. He had the first bedroom. It was only 1' ft smaller than the others. There was a visible silhouette of the creaky staircase that led to the upstairs unit. This made his room appear even smaller.

The entire interior was a basic off white. Mom asked us which paint color we wanted for our bedrooms. There was a beautiful color I did not know the name of at the time. It was a cross between blue and purple. So, I told her I wanted purple or blue. "Don't you like pink," Mom inferred. No, pink is for babies," I said. Are you sure, I like pink for girls and blue is for boys," Mom replied. When it came down to the final decision, Ben ended up with a powder baby blue color bedroom. I ended up with a pink bedroom. Mom and Dad ended up with a rose red bedroom, which showed the best. I was so disappointed. They could have left my room in the plain off white. Ben was thrown off a bit too, a regular blue would have been fine. Maybe Mom wanted to give us the children rooms she always wanted us to have.

We would casually meet other children on our block. They would tell us about all the fun they had in our basement with the former residents. My guess is that they played the doctor game. They were a little brackish because they lost their friends.

After hearing the same story a few times our building was targeted. Pre-teen boys would come and throw eggs at our porch. The eggs mostly hit the ceiling of the porch cover. This would go on about once a week for a few weeks from an unknown enemy. For some reason, the area they hit ended up attracting bees for years.

When vandals wanted to be low down. They would let the eggs rot first then come to throw them. We would be inside minding our business when this would go on. One day these boys boldly decided to throw eggs while Ben and I was standing on the porch. They did not throw at us, they kept aiming for the porch ceiling. Dad must have heard it. He came to the front door with no shoes on. "There they go, those boys are throwing eggs," I yelled. They were standing directly across the street. Dad went and threw on his hardbottom dress shoes that he wore to work every day so fast. I was so afraid for Dad because I did not think he could run in those shoes.

The guys panicked and took off running once they saw my 50 something year old father soaring down the stairs. Ben and I looked on in shock because we never saw Dad so energized, let alone running. I thought for sure those young boys would get away and one did. Dad took those long legs sprinting across the street. He caught one of the boys and held him tight in the back of his collar. The boy was so terrified and apologetic. Dad talked to the boy, while still holding him firmly. He was such an imposing figure with his large hands and booming gravelly voice. He held him up for a few minutes before finally letting him go. After that incident, we had no more problems with people throwing eggs. Not even around Halloween season.

After transferring from Spencer to Lowell Elementary School. I noticed this new school was way behind. There was no class work. In the few months I attended Spencer we would write and work with numbers. At Lowell, the teachers mostly read to us during a half day of school. There were no books readily available.

Every month we were given book order slips to take home. The parents were being pushed to order 3 expensive books monthly. Mom was not onboard with the program. She never purchased the recommended books. Sometimes she would purchase one of the alternative books that were affordable, for a cost under $12. I felt a little left out. But I also felt like it would not have changed anything. It was more so a matter of fitting in. They were not teaching the children how to read. A good majority of the kids did not even know how to tie their shoes or zip their coats. So, in many regards I felt like they needed to catch up to me.

Just before we left Spencer Elementary, Ben would earn all kinds of achievement awards. His teacher tried to get him promoted to skip a grade. After transferring to Lowell Elementary, things were in complete contrast.

At the new school Ben was threatened with a demotion. His new teacher wanted to hold him back in the same grade at the end of the school year. I thought surely there was some mistake. At parent- teacher conferences, teachers informed my parents that Ben seemed to take on a follower role. He gravitated to all the children who were acting out. Year after year, teachers would voice their concerns to my parents about the same thing. They did not think it was something to be majorly concerned about.

Mom would talk to us about being leaders and not followers. I am instinctively a loner. I was considered very shy at the time, but I still had game plans. My peers would always gravitate towards me. I ended up making friends easily because they would approach me. Lucky for me, my friends would be the cool kids, fun and good natured for the most part.

Ben on the other hand, had a harder time with friends. He had some associates, and he was a decent kid. He was laidback, curious and a little mischievous. It's okay to have a partner or running buddy but he always seemed to be searching for the best friend he didn't need. He wanted to fit in. There were a lot of boys on our block alone that were close to his age. Some of them went to private schools. Their parents saw the writings on the walls and just paid the extra money for a better educational experience.

Ben's favorite past-time was to get electronics, take them apart in attempts to create something larger or in his mind better. He wanted to create a massive sound system by using components from different electronics he would find or felt like people were no longer using.

The record player in Mom's jukebox style radio console was not working. The console ended up securing a second life as a tv stand. Ben cut through the wicker woven front covers to remove the speakers and tweeters. He got tools to extract electronic boards. He then fused the wires together to achieve the sound he wanted. Some of his Frankensound projects worked, most did not. Dad in his boisterous cynical voice, would tell him that he was just tearing things up. Ben seemed to embody the notion that he was destroying things. These times could have been coachable moments to take stock in his curiosity. Cultivate his aspirations in working with his hands instead of disparaging him. Mom eventually took notice to the slits in her console and had him put a stop to the destruction as well.

Our cousin Spoony who lived upstairs, was born the same year as Ben. There is nothing better than having a blood relative as a running buddy. It was no matter that they had contrasting personalities. Spoony was very outgoing. He would be the one to get things started. He would come up with silly games to play, tell jokes and pull pranks. There was a legendary story of a 7 year old Spoony at the height of his mannishness. Within an earshot of adults, he would sing a song like Prince's Controversy and change the lyrics to count-your-pussy. Mom would be adult to catch that one. And of course, he would deny it. While at the same time everyone had a good laugh.

One thing I did not understand at the time, but I am glad that it stuck with me. It was Mom's decision to start a small backyard garden. I was born into a regimen that was so disconnected from nature. Weekly trips to the grocery store was the norm. I thought something was wrong with planting seeds in this city soil. I did not think that food would grow. This was before I even knew about pollution and contamination. I thought something was not right about us growing it ourselves.

Mom explained to me that growing our own food was healthier for us. Doing this would also save money on groceries. It did not help that I was a notoriously picky eater. Vegetables had a slim chance of being consumed by me anyhow. She sometimes called me po'. Because she thought I was too small and skinny. It is as if she thought I would succumb to starvation. She would even compare me to the starving children from other countries that were being exploited in tv commercials.

The backyard was set up like a lowercase h. Behind the h was a long strip of land on top of the h was the larger lawn area. We busted up the soil and any grass area along the long strip of land as well as the arc portion under the h.

After hoeing and sifting the soil, we planted the seeds in rows. Mom left the seed packets on sticks at the end of the rows to tell what was growing where. It took a little time for the food to grow. The labor of completing the gardening did not bother me at all, it was fun. The location hindered the kids a little because we used to do flips on the end of the pole frame.

A couple of months passed, by then the food started flourishing. We grew tomatoes, green onions, okra, cucumber, cabbage, mustard, turnip and collard greens. My first introduction to tomatoes were on hamburgers. I did not like tomatoes. I would routinely pull them off my sandwiches. As the tomatoes grew larger, they would sprout up along the cylinder trellis. They first came in green. Mom would pick them, slice them round and season them with cornmeal and fry them.

"Momma, why are your... tomatoes green? What's wrong with them," I asked? I thought I had found my exhibit A on why you shouldn't grow your own food.

"These tomatoes are not ripe, when they ripen, they will turn red. We used to eat these all the time back home. It's called fried green tomatoes. You should try it," said Mom.

"No thank you, I will not be trying any fried green tomatoes. I don't even like regular red tomatoes" I replied.

After I saw Mom eating a few. The aroma was appealing. She ended up breaking a piece off for me. I finally gave it a try. It was a different from anything I had tasted before. Next thing I know, I started running through them, one after the other.

"I thought you didn't like tomatoes," Mom said.

"I don't, but I like fried green tomatoes," I replied.

Some neighbors would come by and ask if they could grab a few ripe tomatoes. Mom didn't mind sharing her bounty. Every now and then a pre-teen would grab a couple to throw at someone.

Our garden only lasted for a couple of years before the project was abandoned. The only thing that continued to grow back was the green onion, which were native to the land. Even after trying actively get rid of them, they came back faithfully like wild weeds.

We were not the only family on the block with food growing in the yard. A family across the street had a pear tree in their backyard. They were generous. Whatever we could not eat, my parents would preserve them for later. Neighbors a few doors down had black and red mulberries growing in their backyard.

We had no idea what they were at the time. Many of us were programmed to believe much of the small growing fruit was poison.

The only time I recall going into their yard was with Ben, my cousins, some friends from the block and the kids who lived there. Half of us were on top of the garage roof daring each other to eat the fruit. A few of them tried the fruit while we monitored to see if they would pass out. Once that curiosity passed, we started a war with the kids on the ground throwing the mulberries around.

Seeing an abandoned shopping cart in a neighborhood can be a sign of bad news. When an empty shopping cart showed up on the neighborhood block it became an opportunity for fun for us. As many kids that could fit in the cart climbed in. A few of the older kids stayed outside the cart to push it. Instead of walking, we would go running up the block depending on how light the cart was. Those who could not fit inside were a little upset that they had to wait. The next time around, I had a turn to get in. The cart was already full, but I could have sat on someone. The cart tilted a few times. But someone was there to level it out. As long as I had waited my turn, I changed my mind. I felt maybe it was best not to join in this time. The kids went marching up and down the street. The cart was super loud every time it hit a crack in the sidewalk because of all the extra weight. Next thing we know, the cart tilted and fell over hard and fast. No one was there to catch the cart from falling over.

Those who were able climbed out. The others who were supposed to guide the cart helped to lift it up. The last kid to get out was Aunt Candi's youngest son, Todd. His arm was twisted and hanging the wrong way. He was a tough kid. He didn't cry. His siblings hesitantly walked him back home to his mom. They knew she would be livid. Aunt Candi brought Todd downstairs to our house for Mom to take a look. They were hoping it was just a sprain. She decided not to chance it and took him to the hospital. The hospital was a neighbor of ours, literally the next building over right across the alley.

Aunt Candi's two daughters were older than me. I would mostly hang with my cousin Ava who was around Ben's age. Her older sister Carla was nearly 10 years older than me. It seemed like the older the kids got, the more freedom they had.

When Ava and Carla would take a walk to the corner stores, I was able to tag along. When they would take their long walk to "The Ave," I had to stay home. If I followed them, Carla was adamant that I needed to go back home. I wanted to know what was next. Where were they going and what were they hiding? They never talked about what they were doing on their new mission.

Carla mostly hung with Tati's older sister. When they were together, Ava had to stay home with us. The Ave was half a mile away. Their high school was located on The Ave. We later learned they had boyfriends who lived around there as well.

Outside of jumping rope, riding our bikes was our favorite pastime. We would ride down all the blocks and alleys within a ¼ mile radius. Some alleys we only rode down a couple of times due to the area being desolate and creepy. Snake alley was one for sure.

After a while, the walking down to The Ave must have become too much for Carla and Tati's sister. They started asking us for a ride on our bikes. It was okay at first. They would take their ride and come right back. Then they got out of hand. They wanted to borrow our bikes almost every day. They even took their precious time, which left us with little to do on the block. It got to the point where they would take our bikes anyway after being told no, by just snatching them from us. It would be nightfall before we saw them again.

We would walk to the corner stores at least once a day. We had about 3 or 4 stores that were nearby. Half of the trips to the store was not even for us. Our parents would have us go on their behalf. The only thing we could not buy was liquor. In addition to small groceries and toiletries, children were able to purchase lottery tickets and cigarettes straight from the corner store. It did not take long to figure out Mom's favorite numbers or her favorite brand of cigarettes. She would change her cigarette brand sometimes. There were even lite versions of cigarettes to try and assist in weening smokers off of nicotine.

We would cut through the alley when we walked in groups for the short route to the store. I was not brave enough to walk through them alone, although I had done it twice. Sometimes Mom and I would walk to the store together, but that was a rare occurrence.

One of the strangest things would happen on our trips to the store. I found it odd even back then and was totally creeped out by it. There would be Spanish speaking men grouped up near the stores who would flirt with us so young. They would get riled up saying things like, "hey, mommy," and other flirtatious words in their language, blow kisses and wink their eyes. I thought they were flirting with my older pre-teen and teenage cousins. I realized they directed their flirtations toward the younger girls as well. It would just be Tati and I as young as 6, 7 and 8 years old with these extra grown men trying to catcall us. Not sure if this behavior could have been bore out of habit or if we were in any true danger. When I would walk there with Mom the energy was different. They would part the way without all that catcalling. They would say things like, "hello ma'am, excuse me ma'am." This lets me know that they knew how to behave but chose not to.

Around our pre-teens, Tati and I started getting around town on our own to small shopping trips on the northside of town. At our age we would have only had to pay half price with a student id which we would not get until high school. Tati's mom worked for the bus company. She gave us bus transfers to get us where we needed to go and back within a reasonable time.

We explored all over the city to some extent. My favorite was downtown Chicago. I ended up choosing to attend one of the few if not the only high schools located in the downtown area. The realities of the big city set in. There were some homeless people who slept outside the entrance of the school. They did not bother us for anything. Most would normally be gone before the start of the school day.

PROTECTION

Simply put children need protection. There is no reason why a child in a two-parent household should feel unprotected. Although, the talk and awareness about a Boogeyman gave credence to the existence of child predators. A figurative character was not the person to watch out for. The reality is, I was solely around family. I wish I knew with certainty, whose identity Mom was protecting. Outside of possible third-party involvement, what else would cause a mother to not step up and be truthful with their own child? Was Mom trying to protect me from myself?

By giving this action a name, I would know exactly what happened. The words rape, sexual assault or molestation would not have clicked until later. Eventually, I would have grown to know why these acts are heavily vilified. Knowing this act was wrong I could have sought out the help and counseling I needed. To keep silent by just ignoring me about that vicious attack can be seen as more of a selfish act. Why hold something so life altering away from a person who is seeking answers? There was extreme avoidance over this issue. Answering questions meant facing facts.

Based on the things that came out of my mouth as a toddler, I don't know how Mom was able to process it. One confession would have driven me straight out. Get the perpetrators jail time. So long as you do what is right, social services and custody should not have been an issue. Handle your business. Who are you protecting? Brother, uncle, cousin, father, I don't care who you are. At what point are they held accountable.

No one paid for their actions that I could attest to. No one ever offered any protection in my younger years. A cousin or two verbally offered themselves up as protectors in my teenage years and I really appreciated them. It helps to have a go to person to count on. Someone who can be there not only to defuse attacks to but someone to act as a dominate negotiator. A person who would make sure that this type of thing never happens again, by no means. Even if the result is just blasting the perpetrators wickedness in the street.

Sex is a normal natural act between two consenting adults. When a child is harmed by sexual acts, this becomes a warped experience that changes the rest of their lives. It is beyond selfish and wicked for a person to rob a someone of their childhood and cause them sporadic stress throughout their lives.

Incest comes into play when you are dealing with sex acts between family. There is no way to normalize any parts of this. That parent may have experienced something similar in their childhood. When their child experiences the same thing, that does not make it okay. It becomes a generational thing when no one puts forth the will to stop. Wrong is wrong no matter the relation.

It is time to have this real conversation and stop joking about that family member who is not quite right. Do not be afraid to have an intervention with that family member everyone has to hold their kids tight around. Let the person know who needs to know that you do not want them picking up your kids or have the kids sitting on their lap. That person may not have even known the family felt that way. Do not keep the secrets. Speak freely, so that the children can live freely.

A discussion would have helped the immensely. My heart, my mind and physical body needed protection. Adults must be watchful of a wandering child. Talk it out. Do not ignore the problem. Give your child full insight on how to navigate when dealing with people. Detail good productive human interaction and inform them on harmful, vicious intent. If something wrong has taken place, empower them with the knowledge of that event at some point in their life. If the parent decides not to start counseling at least allow that child, the choice to pursue it later in life.

A child is just a child. Let them be. Guide them to be respectful. And never take them for granted. This is their foundation you are building. Too many people see these beginning years as some sort of throw away years. These years should be their best years. Instill greatness and provide them with the strongest protection they will ever meet.

Teach and display healthy relationships. From day one, let your child know you are there for them even when they don't see you. Let them know that you will handle anyone who tries to cause them or the family any harm. Tell them, not to fear anything or anyone no matter what a person may say.

There is a tendency to look back over the years to seek out the source of our proverbial scars. We may have emotional, mental or physical scars and we have not a clue of where it all started. There are some who remembers exactly what happened to them. The memory plays it back and it can haunt the mind. Remembrance is the teller. While those holding pain constantly seek a healer.

I cannot say that I was equipped to provide protection for myself. I am sure that I may have crossed paths with the perpetrator again. My safety was compromised by the family not having a real discussion about the wrong that was done.

If you are going to tell a child to be mindful, don't bother with unrealistic figures like a Boogeyman. Start with regular people. Regular folks can be the monsters. Some people carry demons. We all must be aware. Some people switch up their outward persona. For others, from the time you have known them a horrible character is who they always were.

It is an invisible mask people wear. There are occasions that may require a person to display certain demeanor or a higher respectable mannerism. That mask comes on to depict that outer facade to make an impression on others. This portrayal helps people fall in line and buy in to the role of their character.

You may know someone who profess in their adult years that their parents come off one way in public. The parent presents an image that is likable and easy going. Their children later tell, that is what the public saw but behind closed doors that parent did many disparaging things toward them.

By choice and by default, my mother would be my confidante. I then go to examine my relationship with Dad and Ben. Why was it that I never turned to them for protection? That should have been the safe and logical way to go. They should have provided a haven for me. Let it be known to others and myself that they were there for me. As protectors, they should have been the first to know when someone was not treating me right. Family should always be the first line of defense.

There was a feeling of overall safety when we were all together as a family. But protection as a young lady, is something that always felt off.

Going into my teenage and young adult years, Dad's presence was felt by my male friends. Dad had an intimidating presence. No guy that came around ever tried physical harm toward me. Dad was 6' ft tall older salt and pepper haired man with a deep gravelly voice. He paid the bills and took care of home. He had limited interaction with us as children even though he was physically there.

As much as I love Aunt Rosie, after a while I stopped visiting as often. I ended up becoming one of the only female children at the house. There was pretty much nothing for me to do. Now Ben, most likely had a ball. Plenty of the boys were around his age.

One day I sat in a room with a few of my male cousins. They were watching a movie that had a bunch of repetition. I told them, "this is the dumbest movie I ever seen in my life." It was what appeared to me to be, a hot dog and a bun. This hot dog kept being removed and placed back into the bun, over and over again. My guess is that it was some form of softcore porn.

I told Mom about the movie as soon as we got home. I made sure Ben was right there, so that he could get what was coming to him. I was waiting for her to tell someone off. She said it was okay and then said I could use it as a learning opportunity. I was completely shocked. I did not expect that reaction. I stopped visiting Aunt Rosie's house for the most part. Hopefully, she didn't take it personally. This was a step I took in protecting myself.

Around this time an 18 year old neighbor calls my name while I was outside. I turn around. He is clinging to our chain-link gate with his hard penis poking through the hole. Why is he sending a kid these signals?

Naturally, the world of objectification comes to mind. Back in my younger childhood years, the mainstream media would play trailers of X-rated or XXX films. Parents would need to explain to their curious children, the meaning of the X's. Who finally cared to change things?

This took me to reflect on my pre-teen years. I should not have taken in so much hardcore rap music alongside my brother. They would talk about women so horribly. I never wanted to become like those females they rapped about.

I thought the rapper's expression was the same as the mindset of all males. I didn't know at the time that these males were highly exaggerating. Some truth mixed in with a lot of fantasy. These rappers spent a lot of time speaking on another person's experiences. Akin to a pimp for example.

Many of the early hardcore rappers were influenced by pimp or street culture that they may have witnessed in real life or in 'art'. On the flipside, 70's exploitation films glorified pimp culture and the degradation of women. A movie is the story told in action. The music artist rewrites the story. By the time I was born those types of films were on the downtrend, due to a backlash for undermining the community.

Not only was Ben heavily influenced by rap and old school music. He would take in all of the 70's references. He loved embodying of the 70's culture and style. One of the unique styles of the 70's that Ben carried from rap culture was the hair.

When Ben came into his teen years, he became style conscience. He started off with a popular mild relaxer curl kit to style his hair. The mild relaxer curl kit was not as chemically strong as the wet look Jheri Curl. The S-Curl was for shorter hair styles. It gave his hair a shiny, curly, wavy texture. The S-Curl brand name stuck with most with the mainstream, but the brand he preferred to use was the Duke Wavy Curl kit. He sported that style for a while in the early 90's.

But the throwback style he kept the longest was a straighten relaxed hairstyle. This style was popular with West Coast rappers like DJ Quik and Dru Down. He made it his thing. He would reference characters in 70's exploitation films like The Mack as an influence.

Back when Ben and I would have our fighting moments, and there were plenty. I loved when we got along. Maybe, I had a short memory when it came to our fights because I always went back after a day or two. We would get along for a while. He would introduce me to everything hot like new music, games or pop culture styles. We would just hang out and have fun. He had such a great sense of humor that most people wouldn't get to experience unless you are close to him.

I would watch my Saturday morning cartoons and later on pre-teen shows like Saved by the Bell and Hangtime. At 11:00am Ben would emerge from his room to watch Soul Train in the dining room. We would watch our favorite artists or see who the budding new artists were. We would also watch to see if they were up on the new dances. Afterall, the show originated in our hometown. This show was the main thing we agreed on.

Other than that, we would listen to music in his room. I guess he could only tolerate me for about 30 minutes to an hour. After that time, he would be ready to fight. I'm not sure what would trigger him. Or maybe he just didn't want to be bothered with his little sister for long.

There was some sibling rivalry. I really looked up to him. Maybe, my parents didn't introduce him properly to the prospect and reality of having a younger sibling. He always seemed to have some resentment towards me. I did not know what those feelings were at the time.

Our fighting seemed excessive. Other family and friends did not fight with their brothers the same way I did. I wanted my parents to recognize that Ben's behavior was an issue. They mostly ignored my concerns. Sometimes they would yell and tell him to quit. But there was no serious discipline or talks. Ben never got the understanding of why he shouldn't treat me in this way. I don't recall them giving him a lesson on how to treat females with respect. He was never taught to look out for me or to provide a cover of protection. It would have been nice to have someone to turn to when my space was being violated by the local toads.

Our worst fight may have been our last fight. I could not tell what triggered any of them. We were in the dining room. I was sitting in a lounger style chair. He came up to me while I was sitting and started swinging. He would always attack me in his room but never in the dining room where he could be seen or heard by our parents. He hit me in my jaw so hard. I had trouble getting him off me. In the midst of the chaos, I remember thinking that Ben had lost his whole mind. Not only that, he clung to me fighting like a feral cat.

I had to strategize quick. Then I remembered, Mom had bought this huge white and gold antique phone from a garage sale. To our surprise the phone still worked. That phone sat on a stand right next to the chair. Ben had gotten really cozy in his attack and kept on going. Once I got him on a good angle, I grabbed the phone and hook with a firm grip. With as much energy as I could muster, I swung that phone hard and swift to his head. I tried to knock him flat out. This was the only thing that got him to stop.

He finally backed up off of me. I have no idea where our parents were at the time. They were home but not inside of the house. Moms favorite place was outside on her the covered front porch. As soon as I saw her, I let her know what happened. I also told her that I believed that my jaw was broken. Ben was given the same dry, "don't do that to your sister."

My main issue was my jaw. It hurt so bad especially when I tried to eat and talk. I was ignored. Mom would tell me, there was nothing wrong with my jaw and that it will be alright. The pain went on for over a month. I informed her weeks later that I was still in pain. I never went to the hospital for it. One reason they avoided the hospital was because they never had medical insurance for me. Mom had a medical card for Ben and herself. Dad had insurance for himself through his job. Time only healed my jaw injury.

One of my favorite things about growing up was getting an allowance. Dad came around like clockwork with our allowances. It was small, just a couple of dollars every week but it was like a payday for us. Honestly, I can say that it was unearned. My parents did not give us scheduled chores and they did not come down hard on us about homework. I never felt pressured to have the best grades in school. I admit that there were times I received some grades that I was not proud of. But none of that stopped my weekly pay.

After so long, I got tired of spending my money on the same things every week. I asked Mom, "what if I saved my allowances instead of spending." She applauded it. "That is a great idea," Mom cheerfully replied. That was all the encouragement I needed. I was curious about watching my money grow.

Mom had given me a small red zipper coin purse a while back. That is where I kept my allowances. I kept it in the house and only took out the money I needed when I wanted to spend. Everyone knew that coin purse was mine. Outside of keeping it in my room. I thought it would be fun to choose a place to hide it where no one would think to look. I chose the next small room over, the pantry. I hid that little red bag behind my favorite spot, the cookie jar.

I had no idea that there would be eyes on me there. My money started to build for weeks. I thought it would take forever. Surprisingly, I did not break down to start spending again. Next thing I knew, I had four weeks' worth of allowances saved. I was so excited and shared the news with Mom. She was so proud of me.

Not long after stacking those allowances. I went to check on my money in its special building place. My little red coin purse was discarded off to the side. The contents were emptied out. I could not believe that all my saving effort was gone so quickly. Not only that, if the money were to be spent, I should be the person to enjoy it. That was the most disappointing of it all. It took a change in spending habits and patience to get there.

After asking around in frustration and tears. Ben pretended to know nothing. Our parents questioned and pressured him. Finally, the truth comes out. He had taken the money and used it for himself. No parts were returned. According to him, he had spent it all. There was no regard for me, his sister.

The same way 'I love you' was rare in our household, so were apologies. If a person never has to admit their wrongdoing, never remorseful or ever held accountable for anything, then what have you learned? Ben was allowed to run amuck.

One day Tati and her big sister came our house crying. This was so odd. They had never come to our house to speak to Mom before. They had run into Ben around the corner from the house. Apparently, Ben had slapped my friend so hard it left a handprint on her face. She was still crying hysterically by the time they got to our house. They had been our next-door neighbors for many years. We were so close to their family that she should have been like a little sister to him as well.

He had the potential to be a good guy and for the most part he is. He just always had a mischievous streak. Something was going on with Ben. My family passively missed so many signs. The worst part being Ben joining a gang because they told him they would be his family. Shortly thereafter he started dabbling in drugs.

Our parents were there physically and financially. Mom only worked when Dad had extensive hospital stays. Dad left the workforce early after his health issues he was considered disabled. So, they both were around for the most part. But you must pay attention to your children and constantly communicate. The lack of communication and expression of feelings really hurt our family dynamics.

The fractures created over time in our childhood grew into some form of brokenness amongst us.

As man and wife, it was difficult for me to see how my parents related to each other. They kept things fairly peaceful in front of us. They tried their best not to argue or fight in front of us. There were a few disagreements that were squashed quickly between them. They fought a time or two behind closed doors. But we could hear it. We saw the aftermath of their bedroom in disarray looking like a tornado hit it.

We never saw affection between them as a married couple. I often wondered how we got here. Obviously, marriage is no fairy tale. But gives us something loving as a model that we could follow for when we get older.

Other than their interaction, they had a traditional marriage. She was a stay at home mom who cooked, cleaned and looked after the children. He was a provider, home protector and kept up the maintenance.

As tough as Mom was, I still had to ask myself was Mom passive when it came to incidents of abuse? I also thought about the other side of the coin. Was there something lacking in the leadership on Dad's part? Is this the reason why I felt that I could not go to him for help?

TRUTH BEING BONDAGE

HEAVY ANGST

The kids would group up for our usual walk home. One day, a horrifying event had taken place at an elementary school in Winnetka, IL. We were totally unaware. Mom and Aunt Candi met us at the door with big hugs and I love you. We all had the strangest looks on our faces. We were totally confused. What has gotten into these women?

Just like my parents, Aunt Candi rarely openly displayed affection for her kids as well. We didn't think much of it. That's just how things were.

Another rarity were my parents. I have never seen my parents deal with each other in an affectionate way. Some adults think no, let's not do that in front of the children. We did not see any kisses, no hugs and never witnessed an, I love you. I never even seen them reach out to hold hands. The most affection I saw was them stand together to take a picture. He put his arm around her. This simple gesture had my mind blown. Their loving ways and intimacy were scant at best from what I saw from my parents. They were overly discreet.

Interacting with others helped to shape my overall perspective. My friend Tati is one of the biggest social butterflies I have ever known. She was always doted on. She was free with her affection and friendships. Her family made me question if anything had been missing in relation to my own. She would call elders her auntie or uncle, even if they were not related. That was just unheard of to me. She was the first person to show me what a godmother was. She would get gifts from her even when it wasn't a special occasion. She got them just because they loved her. I eventually went home to have a talk with Mom to find out if I had a godmother. "You don't have one. You don't need one. Am I not enough for you" Mom said? She had a point. Mom really was all that I needed.

I would be remised not to notice that our home carried an energy. It was so thick. There was a heavy angst. At the time, I was clueless as to where this feeling came from. At least now, I have a couple of guesses and I still may be wrong. There were many days I felt like I was walking on eggshells. It was like a void. As if something was missing. Well welcome home. It is what, it is. Just keep it moving and hopefully it will dissipate someday.

Did either one or both of my parents have resentment for us? I later learned Mom wanted a singing career. Surprised, is how I felt to learn this. Seeing that she barely hummed around the house. One day I heard her singing. "Oh, my goodness, what are you doing? You can't sing," I immediately expressed! The look of shock was on her face.

"Really, I was always told that I had a beautiful singing voice. People told me to keep singing so I wouldn't lose my voice," said Mom. She paused to look at her hand, she said, "it could be these cigarettes too."

"Whatever it is, you don't need to sing anymore," I replied.

I was not being malicious. The youth will give you brutal honesty. I am glad to say, that I survived the encounter and still standing to tell the story. She appreciated my brutal honesty.

One Saturday morning, I overheard a conversation Dad was having with one of his work buddies. "If I didn't have these kids here, I would be in a senior building too," said Dad. That is when I figured that I had found the director of angst.

In his defense, that was a conversation between two grown people. He probably paid no mind to me in the room watching a show that Saturday morning. Maybe Dad told his buddy that to make him feel more comfortable about his new accommodations in his senior apartment. But as a kid I thought, he really does not want to be here with us.

Locating the energy source of this angst was taxing. I hoped to be able to cut through it someday. I felt freer to express myself in a more playful manner when Dad was not home. It was party time! Most children probably feel this way when their father is away.

Living around a person for any amount of time you learn how to deal with them. You learn what tends to aggravate them as well as how to get to their good side. I learned what things I could come to Dad with that would keep him less fussy. Dad was only okay with me asking for money or when something needed fixing. In between our weekly allowances he had no problem giving us some change or a few dollars in the meantime.

My parents had an agreement that only Mom would be the disciplinarian. She did not allow Dad to whoop us. I don't know if that was based on something that happened in the past with Ben or based on something that happened with her own father. She thought that he would be too rough with us.

Her weapon of choice was one of Dad's old belts. Some frayed old leather strap. She was so adept with her whooping technique that she really did not need a belt. Her hands felt about the same if not worse. She likely saved herself some pain from impact by using the belt.

It's not like I got whooping's for no reason. I usually knew when they were coming. I tried to talk her out of them. As I grew a little older, I had a revelation.

It all came together one day when Mom cornered me into the bathroom. I melted down to the floor near the door. She had the belt and her arm raised. Then she commences the butt whooping. All while it was going on, I started to think outside of the whooping. I thought why are we doing this? Enough already! I was tired of getting a lick for each word she would speak. Not only was there a lick for each word. It was more so a lick for each syllable in the word. I thought about how silly this was. Next thing I know, I just started laughing. I laughed hysterically. It still hurt, but I refused to give her anymore tears. I am not crying anymore! And dare I ask, "IS THAT ALL YOU GOT"?! Nah, I would not play with her like that.

Clearly, she thought I had lost my mind. The intimidation was over. I won that fight. That was my last whooping. I only wish I had laughed sooner.

As a pre-teen, Mom turned to have disdain toward me. It was just a matter of existence. I could be plating my dinner from the stove. She would snarl at me and say, "with your fast ass." I had no idea what she was talking about. This had become a daily taunt. What does being 'fast' even mean? This came out of nowhere for no reason. Maybe it was due to my feminine development starting. That was something outside of my control. It is a natural part of life. I was not around any boys hugging, holding hands, kissing on them, grinding or being sneaky. If I was not in the house with her, I was outside with my friends. This horrible label hurt me to the core. All I could think was you used to be nice to me. You used to love me. She suddenly changed with no warrant.

In school, I was not the greatest student. Not because I could not be. I did not have the patience for the curriculum. Reading 30 to 40 pages for homework of five to six courses just to answer six to ten questions at the end of the chapter was not my idea of learning. Most of the subject matter barely held my attention span.

After a while, I was ready to zoom to high school graduation so that I could leave home. I was tired of this off feeling that came with being at home. When the tv show A Different World came around it was encouragement. It made me want to do better in school as well as learn more about HBCU's. The future prospect of college was a positive future outlet. I had made up my mind just as I was approaching my teenage years that I was going to college. My plan included going to school out of state.

I couldn't wait to tell Mom about my future plans. We sat on the sofa one day and I told her what I planned to do. "You want to leave me," she reacted. This took me back a bit. It was not about leaving her. I thought she would have been proud. "We have plenty of time to be together. I have not made it to high school yet," I reminded her.

After Dad's health issues and early retirement, maybe there was marital or financial stress. Monthly checks were probably too tight to budget. Adjusting to a budget had to be a challenge. Mom told me that she had to borrow money from Aunt Lee a couple of times. She showed me where she had to send higher payments off to the mortgage company to catch up on back payments. When they first purchased the building there were some economic challenges going on in the country. They ended up with a ridiculously high 18.5% interest rate. They had not refinanced that original interest rate at that time.

Whatever the cause was, that feeling of angst just hoovered and remained in the home unfortunately.

CHAPTER 10

PLAYING THE BACKGROUND

On an unconscious level events in my life had a major effect on my character. I am a laid-back person that avoided attention. I believe that I would have been this way to some extent, regardless of circumstances. There is nothing wrong with this. The only problem is, when you are kind of quiet and mostly to yourself, it brings about curiosity in others. People approach you and want to know more about you. Most times you may be approached in a respectful manner. Some are not so respectful.

There are times when I felt no need to add something more to a conversation being had. And that is okay. Why ramble just to ramble? Unfortunately, some people will label you as stuck up. Or people question, do you think you are better than everyone else. When this is not the case. Especially after having my space violated. I cannot be everything to everybody. I am very vigilant about where I spend my time and energy.

I never understood why people who made grand entrances or the type who make it a point of having their voices heard would be the main people concerned about my participation. It was as if they had deep desire to make my presence known on my behalf. I call it fronting me off and I don't care for it. No need to bring me anything extra. If I need attention, I know how to garner that for myself.

There is an axiom saying that you have to watch those quiet ones. That can be true in some cases. Attention seekers normally tell on themselves and take all the guess work out. The truth is, you better watch everyone if that is the case. People will show you what they want you to see. There is a reason why people fall for conmen and master manipulators. They can focus in on an image or a certain look of how they need to present themselves. They can also focus in on buzz words, mannerisms or anything revolving around what makes you more agreeable to their agenda.

I am pretty much what you see is what you get, with even more treats inside. The only problem is, I cannot say with certainty if I have let anyone inside. I don't have a hard exterior. And I am no big softie either. Sometimes people find it hard to approach me because they don't know what I am thinking. I treat everyone in a fair manner. Once a person gets past their own preconceived thoughts, they soon learn the approach was much easier than they thought it would be.

I was labelled as shy. I did not mind this label because it seemed fitting in my childhood years. Quiet and shy was my description. I always felt there was more to me than just that.

Having to look out for my own protection I became keen on discernment. It's one thing to see what people are presenting. As they call it, their representative. You should look out for angles. A position can be used to get closer to fulfill their personal agendas. Nonverbal communication can be just as telling. Watch how a person move as well as examine their character. There are times I do not catch it all. Fortunately, I have been able to snuff out many storms that were brewing.

My critical thinking skills would go into overdrive. All the questions a child asks are valid. At some point, it is as if we are shunned for taking a second look into things after a certain age. We are groomed to just accept everything we are presented, with no further questions. These days using your brain makes you a troublemaker. It's a real go along to get along mentality. If beholding to deceit and lies is important to you keep it but keep that over there. I will continue to examine all people, places and things that impact my life.

I like dealing in the truth. I could care less about some fancy character someone made up or has modeled themselves after. That is cute and all, but what happens when you can no longer keep up the façade? Who will you become? Do you even know the real you?

I could imagine that Mom thought I was too young to know the truth about what happened to me. At what point do you come clean. There is never an easy time for something of that nature. That memory eventually disbanded from my mind, but it never really went away.

There are some parents out there who are not forthcoming about being true blood relatives. Just because you accept a child as your own, regardless of the arrangement made between the other adult does not mean that the child does not deserve to know. If the true parent has no plans of stepping up, waiting until adulthood maybe best. But don't go on without ever revealing it. They may not care and appreciate the fact that you were there throughout the years. I know a couple of people who have dealt with hidden facts like this. It's best to come clean. In the process set your own heart free. Be there for them the same way you always were.

Trying make sense of life. I could not understand why I was harmed. This was a direct attempt to take away power when it comes to my comfort, sense of protection and self-esteem. This event was like low background music that always played somewhere in the recesses of my mind. This undercurrent affected how I dealt with people.

In an unconscious way, I felt the need to prove to people that I was a good person. So, there was no need to harm me because I would never harm you. I could not understand what I did to deserve what happened to me. I lived on edge for a while. Not knowing when there would be a next time.

I would be good. I was too good, overly good. In many cases, being good to people who did not deserve it. It had gotten to the point that the things I do approached a perfectionist level. Being a perfectionist was not my goal. I had come to the frame of mind that I could not leave anything undone. Everything must be done right. Sometimes while participating in groups,

I would not give input based on the slight prospect I would be wrong.

Avoiding attention by fading into the background wasn't a hinderance to me socially. Luckily, I had enough friends and male companionship into adulthood. It was made easy because people came to me. In my shy days, I could be in room of one thousand people and not say a word to one person unless they came to me first. At the time, I did not know where this social anxiety came from. Since this mannerism had a name, shy, I did not question it much. Naturally, I wanted to know why I seemed to be the only one amongst my family and friends who had this condition. This unique trait inadvertently caused me to stand out.

In my pre-teen and teenage years, I needed protection. I was pestered a lot by my male peers which caused me some scale of depression. There was one guy that would run up on my friends and me. We would be in a group of about 5 or 6. The times he was with his friends, they would try to steal our snacks as soon as we left the store. He would run up on me particularly. He came up a few times on our way walking to school and a few times on the way back home. I did not know his name and at no point did he ask mine. He would grab me and feel up every crevice of my body for his own personal pleasure. I felt so disgusted and humiliated. No one helped.

I was confused as to why he chose me out of the crowd just to violate me. I had no idea who this guy was and I hated him. My friend Faith had a major crush on him and longed for his attention. I told her what he would do to me and how I felt about him, but she didn't care, she was infatuated. She pursued him for a good while, but things never quite came together for them.

Carrying yourself as a person of good character does not always equal to you receiving good treatment in return. The best way to describe me after a while was introverted or ultimately aloof. I noticed that a level of apprehension would come over me when the possibility of dating came around. I had a leg that would stiffen sometimes when walking past multiple men at once. When this temporary paralysis occurred, I would not tell anyone. I hoped no one would notice, especially the guys.

The most attractive and sought-after guys would pursue me. My body matured way before I did. The good thing is, I reinforced my own common sense and thought beyond what I saw on the surface. There are people who only go by what they see visually. I cannot help but feel as though potential suitors never looked beyond the surface of who I am.

There was a time when I started to resent being described as sexy for the mere fact that the word sex is in it. Sex is insinuated. Sexy can be seen as a means to objectify a person. I also understood that sexy is also a good means to attract a potential mate. I was always fully aware that lust and sex were one thing. Neither of them equates to love.

I have had my share of dates where I found myself doing more hand removal and swatting than I cared to. Dating especially in the beginning stages would have been the best time for me to do my best extrovert impression. Distract a date with interesting conversation to get sex off the brain. Then again, if it takes a bunch of distractions to keep a person in line, you may be out with the wrong person regardless. Be conscious about the character of the person you choose to share your time with.

MO ABBIE

CHAPTER

11

UNCOVERED MEMORY

After being Midwest Chicagoland area pretty much my whole life. I had been contemplating a change for a while. As early as my teen years, I knew that I wanted to settle in somewhere else. My wish was that it would be a location with a nice scenery, warmer stable weather, economic opportunities, entertainment and recreation options. A place that could provide a good quality of life. After all, Chicago was starting to change and not for the better.

The urge to relocate became stronger. By this time, both of my parents had passed away. Most of the family I have there is extended. I could come back to visit them whenever the need would arise. There was not much tying me to the area. The wintertime can be brutal and there are parts of the summertime that rivals the brunt of winter.

We had a lot of fun growing up in Chicago. There is always something to do. If you are having dull moments there, it is self-imposed. Letting go of the fun was the hardest thing to do. The people there, family and friends were easy to enjoy. Everyone seems to have a natural sense of humor. You can cross paths someone for a couple of minutes and share a moment that you will tell for a lifetime.

Chicago is definitely not some dream world utopia. It is a bunch of different things. There was always components of crime, drugs and other grimy things. The difference is those elements were more concentrated or targeted. There were more safe spaces. Bad guys went after bad guys, for the most part.

In more recent times, the elements of crime had been deconcentrated around the city leaving no clear target. No neighborhood was immune to some level of crime like it had been in the past. There are areas that still exist where crime is less likely to happen. The gun play is the worst. Children are losing their lives to bullets. There is no place for this, and it will never be normal. Bullets flying wildly through the city put so many people at risk.

The game of life can be a monster in a city like Chicago. Young black males have it the worst. Influence will game up on them strong. Parents, loved ones and friends have to school young men on societal ills early in life. Always keep a positive word for them because they are inundated with negative messages that is intended to knock them off track.

Do your best to instill a moral code in them. Everything you see and hear is not good for you. There will be masses going in one direction. That does not automatically mean it is the right direction. Guide them in the direction of common sense.

It was tough witnessing a few of the young men I had known get caught up on that wrong path to entangle their lives in drugs and the criminal system. Fortunately for them, they still have a chance to turn their lives around. Those who lives were cut short can only be memorialized.

The final decision to relocate came when viewing a two-flat building like the one I had grew up in. The owner selling the property took us up to her unit on the second floor. It was mostly packed up and cleared out. She had a picture of her children in the built-in bookcase. She said that she had decided to move due to the loss of her children. They appeared to be young adults or in their late teens. There was one young man sitting at the table. She said that he was her only surviving son. She lost three of her four sons. My mind staggered.

I had questions. But I did not want to come off as insensitive to a grieving mother. I can only speculate on her decisions as to why it would take her so long to make a move. Her roots may have been deep in the city. Maybe she did not want to leave those connections.

People are losing their families to violence. It takes a certain awareness to navigate large cities. Following the common themes and actions of the masses can send you so far off in the wrong direction. It takes a strong mind to head off your own way when everyone around you are doing something else.

No one wants to stand out. No one wants to go through the task of explaining their actions each time they set out to do something. It is best to just do those things that will uplift you in the long run. Take the action first, fill people in later if it is necessary for them to know.

Sometimes people that you hold dear can be the ones knowingly or unknowingly set up mental roadblocks. They tend to think about what your success means for them. Will your relationship still be close? Will you cut them off? Do they feel the need to compete? It is a good thing to have support, but your success does not need applause or the ego stroke. You need no one to stand in the way of progress. If they want to support you, great! If they choose not to support you, it should have no bearing on what you set out to do for yourself.

After more contemplation, I decided to make a move. I wanted to find a place that was smaller than such a large city as Chicago. It is currently the third largest city in the USA and has been for a good while. A rural setting would be too much of an extreme change. I was familiar with these areas from our visits to the south. Before setting in on a location, I visited several mostly southern cities swinging from Virginia to Texas. I gathered notes on what I liked and did not like.

My hopes were to land on a place that had good weather year-round or at least milder winters. More greenery and less concrete were desired. A few hills would be nice considering how flat Chicago was. A scenic waterway is always appealing. The housing stock that is intact and affordable was a plus. A thriving downtown, entertainment and sporting options had to exist in this prospective town.

I visited the places that I felt could be a good place to settle. The place that felt the most like home or the place that piqued my curiosity the most would be it. I ended up with a couple of maybe cities. Some of the places I really hoped to like, but once I got there, they didn't make the cut. I even hoped to move closer to family in the Carolina's, but it was too rural. The amenities were spread apart miles out.

One year, I had gone down to South Carolina to attend my cousins' funeral. Cousin Lori was one of Mom's two closest cousins. Her two youngest daughters were closer to my age. We are also double cousins. Two family members married two family members of another family. No one was interrelated.

My cousins told me that they never got visitors to come down from the north, unless it was a rare family reunion being held there. Luckily, I had gone down to visit a few years prior. I was able to speak to Lori before she passed. She told me that Mom, Aunt Lee and herself had a singing group. She said that Mom had a beautiful singing voice. I had no idea. They did not make a major push for stardom. It was more like a hobby. The story gave me a bigger picture of Mom. I knew she would draw and paint occasionally. The singing brought it all home. She was a true artist. It was great to spend that time with Lori since I had not seen her in years. It was a treat when they would stay with us when they were in town.

They lived right on the state boarder across Georgia. The evening after the funeral we had gone to downtown Augusta GA, near the Riverwalk. There were a bunch of clubs along the strip. We finally landed on one. We stayed there most of the night. One of my cousins even jumped into the middle of a fight to break it up. She did not know the women. She even pulled one to the side and gave her a pep talk.

We left the area not long after that. We went back to the town that they grew up, in South Carolina. It was a more intimate setting. It was like a house with a bar in it. From the looks, it appeared to be recently remodeled. I was told that it was a store in the daytime hours.

After listening to a few songs and drinking a few drinks. I needed a nap. Everyone was not ready to leave at the time. So, I headed to the car to stretch out. I shut my eyes and dozed off for a while. When I peeped up, there was a large blaze straight ahead toward the bar. Panicking I tried to call and kept calling to reach relatives inside. I relayed the information about the blaze. She said that's just how they get rid of trash sometimes. You would either haul your trash and pay someone to dispose of it or burn it. That is more manual labor for trash than what I am used to.

After that I had just about given up on my quest to leave the Chicago area. Then randomly I took a weekend to visit a city and state I honestly had no previous desire to visit. I researched resident commentary and various stats. The data came back fairly positive. I headed out and looked around town. It felt cozy and quaint. Not too large, not too small. It was also surprisingly clean. One of the cleanest cities I had ever seen for a place that size. That was not on my original checklist, so I gave the area a big bonus for that.

Watching the news later that evening. The forecast predicted freezing rain changing over to snow for the following day. Since I drove that trip, I got up early that Sunday morning to head back home. This place ended up standing out. There was no professional sports team, but they had collegiate level teams that were supported on a diehard fan level. There was no major waterway but there were a couple of small rivers and fishing holes available.

I never thought that I would even remotely think of being in the area for an extended amount of time let alone make this place my home. This place was Kentucky. It was fairly easy to navigate. I expected to have some home sickness. It never came. Discovering things that existed in this new area keep my attention.

As a bit of time passed as a single woman, I noticed there was a major contrast when it came to dating. It was a task to catch the attention of a potential suiter. That was something I had not given a nano second of thought. I always met decent men with ease. In honesty, I wanted a temporary break from dating. About 3 or 4 months of a break would do. That is what I envisioned.

Did I suddenly miss a step? I suddenly became invisible. There was a lot of interracial coupling. For some reason, I did not expect to see that. It was not a common theme back home. When I went would go back home the men were back to flirting. Anytime I would cross state lines into any state for that matter, men would flirt. This was the oddest phenomenon of attraction I had ever experienced.

There were also couples in the town who had been together since they were in middle or high school. From what I observed most people did not venture outside of their core circles much to meet new people. There were also women who were in marriages and long-term relationships who bared the load of household expenses. All they required of their men were to pay an optional amenity of something like the cable bill. These men would be actively working and earning more, but his income is for himself. This nonsense was so rampant. If that is how things are around here, let me tap out in advance.

After talking to a co-worker, she tried figuring out the problem. Why was I single? Being well aware of the area we agreed on local dating dilemmas as she had friends who dealt with similar issues. She even took on the role of the pursuer in her own marriage. Her boyfriend at the time was on the heels of a breakup from an interracial relationship before they got serious. His ex-girlfriend's family disapproved of him. She goes on to say, have you ever thought the problem was you? I told her yes. I did not look past myself as if I am perfect in any way. I had given myself a self-assessment analysis. She seemed surprised that I had already arrived at that conclusion. The analysis I rendered on myself was that I had some walls up and did not freely let people in.

I decided to take on the challenge of reviewing my life. I was excited about combing over my relationships. There were only two relationships I would consider serious. Also taking the time to comb over situations with each person I dated to pinpoint any missed opportunities.

This examination idea came from watching tv shows using psychiatry. I can say this was one benefit I got from it. They would always say, think back. I figured there was no need to seek the help of a therapist when all I had to do was reminisce.

Concluding my thought exercise analysis, everything came back clean. As much as I wanted to blame an ex for doing me wrong and trust me there was plenty of wrong done. I gathered enlightenment about those relationships.

The men I had dated had a fair opportunity. The men I were interested in were put on notice. If they were slow to act, I would only take my advancement so far. If there was no mutual advancement, we would end things there. I am a whole entire person, there will be no extraction of self. Take all of me or none at all. That is my point of view.

As far as those relationships go, I'll just say that we were not on the same page at the same time. Both were mentally and emotionally abusive. No man ever had the gall to cross me on a physical level. My father's presence in my life was my protection. Some guys said they believed my father would shoot them. At the time, I didn't even know that my father had a gun. But they knew.

Even in that abuse, I would not say they are bad people. Something was a bit off, but I could not identify what it was exactly. They were just not for me. It is what I have learned to be flaming narcissism. I added the flaming part. They were characters who never took the time to get to know me. They charmed my family and friends with their polished act. I saw through it as such. At the same time, I did not want to miss out on love if it was the real thing.

My family championed these guys. Their biggest fan would be Dad. The guys I liked the most my Dad did not care for. The ones who were putting on a show, he adored. His co-sign prompted me to move in closer in those relationships. They entertained themselves in my Dad's approval. After all, they would stop by to visit him regularly. Dad would try to get them to do the right thing, but they were just stringing the both of us along.

I will let them slide on by in this moment. A relationship cannot work with one person being 100% real and the other vacillating somewhere between 27 and 43%. The breakups were not dramatic. I was asked by those men to get back together at certain points. One pursued me for years, the other hoovers me on the social media I rarely use.

I have no regrets about any past relationships. They were life lessons. I believe there is a genuine love out there. It is best not to force relationships. When it is your time for love, you will know.

Neatly enough, my research was done. There were no major issues in my relationships. They did not alter the person I am in any negative way. So, I decided to take things a step further. I decided to look way back. That is when I dove back into my childhood. This is the moment I started to uncover my repressed memories.

My mind automatically suppressed and hid away certain memories purposely. That is trauma. The memories came back slowly. I never saw myself as a person who had experienced severe trauma. At the young age when it happened, I knew nothing of what an attack was. The energy and act remained regardless of what my mind blocked. Unwanted attacks can plant a seed of anger.

People would have conversations around me. They would ask others, why I was so quiet. The other person would reply on my behalf, oh she has always been quiet, or she's just shy. Some people would just let that be. Others would go a step further and say, well you know when a person is quiet like that something really bad happened to them. I overheard this a few times in my life but, I never thought deeply about it. I would say to myself nothing happen to me without a second thought. There was also a part of me that wanted to deeply ponder if something traumatic had happened. But I would let it go. I did not want to be "one of those people."

Who are those people? People who have been victimized. Someone who is just minding their own life and others simply

TRUTH BEING BONDAGE

define you by that traumatic incident. When they see you or bring you up, they lead by describing that incident. This can implicitly strip away your identity over and over again. When they can just call you by your name or find new and positive works to identify you by.

For obvious reasons, no one wants to be a victim. Once a person with bad intentions finds out that you have been victimized, they may try to find ways to perpetuate or exploit that trauma. They figure that you have gone through it before, so they pile on. Or you have forgiven trauma in your life. The next time, they may want to turn things up a notch. Sometimes broken people are targeted in their broken state in attempts to get an opportunity to break them down even further. This level of victimhood is also associated with weakness. Most people no matter their circumstance ideally would like to be seen as strong and persevering.

For the sake of argument and the sake of truth, it happened. That traumatic experience happened, and it happened to me. It is what it is. I say it in this way not to be passé or flippant about it. I say it this way in order for me to let go of the shame. That ordeal does not define me in any way. Although, the memory revealed itself later in life. I do not care who knows or what anyone has to say. I am not defined by the sick actions of another individual. Life goes on for me. No matter how hard that person tried to break me. I picked up the pieces at a young age. As much of the truth was hidden from me, I live.

Uncovering these memories, uncovered my truth. I only accept it due to the fact that it cannot be undone. The minute you turn your back, anyone can ensue bad intent on to you or your family. It may even be a member of your family. That is the most heartbreaking part. There was basically only family around.

The incident I experienced with the older man totally devastated me. I buried it. Either way you handle those situations. Thinking about it nearly every day or burying it somewhere in the far recesses of your mind. That can take a toll on you mentally and emotionally. Back then, there was some consciousness on my part building that older people were presumed to be wiser. An older person should be life experience teachers who help you in your growth, learning and wellbeing.

Unfortunately, there are folks who enter their elder years and still want to live as if they are in their youth. They act as if they have not been made wiser over time. They just do what they want to do. They don't care who they hurt. It is a sad state of affairs when people of a certain age cannot be referred to as elders. Still carrying themselves in a predatory manner. Hoping to take advantage of a person's vulnerability. Instead they become widely known as creeps. What a dishonorable way to live.

The bedding incident came to the forefront as well. Up until recently, far into my adult years. I did not know what that experience was. I asked Mom up until I was about 9 or 10 years old. I would ask her: do you remember that time when…? Remember what I told you…? What was that? Whenever I brought it up, it was met with silence. When I was younger, I did not pay attention to the fact that my mother intentionally avoided that question. All I knew was that I never got answers. Around that age, I made that the last time I asked. I said to myself, she is never going to answer me. So, I left it alone.

I did not think about that situation again. I knew something wasn't right. Mom was always responsive and attentive whenever we needed it. For some reason she refused to have that conversation with me. Once the recovery of this memory came along, I started putting the pieces together.

Realizing that I was brutally raped in my toddler years was extremely unsettling. Back then, I did not have the words to define what I had gone through. That is what I wanted. Give me the name of what it was that happened. Give me the name of the person who did it. I used to want to know why. Now knowing there is no justifiable answer for why. Just know that it was done by an ill individual.

This was deep seeded anxiety I carried for a long time. Being made to believe that I was just naturally shy. It was the lie of my life that I had never known. It makes you wonder how many other lies has played on in the background of your life that you are not privy to.

This explains why I have been so guarded throughout my life. Sometimes you find that you are not just living freely. Sometimes you have to fight. You must guard yourself from trespassers. Especially, when your personal space has been violated before. The circumstances that comes along with being violated, becomes now everyone is seen as a potential violator. At least, until trust is earned otherwise. I do not hold all men accountable for the misdeeds of a few. There are good men out there.

I use this experience as a guide moving forward. Strong discernment is always put into play. I can forgive myself for the times I felt as though, I was not totally present in the moment. Or, leading myself into thinking that I could have done more.

My focus has changed and look forward to approaching new relationships with a better sense of self.

I am fortunate and express gratitude for being able to fight like hell for my life as a young toddler. It took so much energy and it still affects me to this day. There are times my energy feels depleted, it is no match to my fortitude that will not be defeated.

WHO KNEW, WHO KNOWS

A feeling of being kept down or suppressed can be hard to shake. It could just be a feeling. It can also be a force field of energy, that can keep us bound. The energy of a negative situation can hold you hostage. Remembrance of a negative act can trigger PTSD.

A feeling of brokenness has traced and followed me as far back as I can remember. Putting situations away just about as soon they happened became common place for me. I shared what needed to be shared with the person who matter most. This person being my Mom. Whether anything was done with the information, I do not know. I really have no way of finding out either. I asked questions that she chose not to answer. If I were speaking on something that was totally out of line, she would not have hesitated to send me away for nonsensical talk. Instead, I stayed around with no answers given.

The wool was pulled over my eyes once again. Mom kept me from the truth. I knew in my spirit that some things going on in my early years didn't seem right. It for damn sure did not feel right. Finally, being able to put the pieces together sent me into another level of life examination.

The people I had known all my life, my designated protectors left a void. I have no bad feelings toward them. It just makes you wonder to what degree do parents and caregivers protect. Also, who do they side with when these omissions are made. An attacker was protected from what I see.

After snatching the lid off of this repressed memory, one of the first things I wanted to know was who did this. I have a short list of suspects. Both of my parents passed away by the time this memory resurfaced. I would have gone to them first about this as an adult looking them eyeball to eyeball. The ignore and let it blow over game ran it's course.

A dose of shame may have set in. Initial panic about who knew about this had overcome me. From my perspective the family gave me strange love. I felt as if something happened that everyone tried to keep from me. Our family is known to associate things to certain family members. If that person is on drugs heavy, watch your things around them. That person has kids and does not have custody of them. Is that true, something you heard or are they co-parenting? They can make up a story. Deem it to be true and run with it.

One of aunts made me feel a certain way. Whenever there was a large gathering, she would make it a point to call me out from all the other family members that were around. She would tell others who I was, and I would speak to the people. In most cases, the people would not speak back. They would just look. As if I was the live action visualization of a story that was narrated by her, once upon a time. I didn't care for it because I don't like a lot of attention.

I am sure those horrible events I experienced in my early years is what's behind me avoiding attention. I didn't want to catch some creeps' eye. Creeps be gone! I literally tried to be as quiet and invisible as possible. I had no idea this behavior is desired by the molesters of the world. They want to destroy lives and they want you to keep their secret.

So, my answer as to who knew, who knows? I only told Mom. I don't know if she shared this information. I thought about who in her circle of family she would have told. Two of her cousins maybe, but they have since passed as well. I thought about asking my aunts. I was still in a protective mode and not wanting to discuss this with many people. Getting the answers I wanted without a huge grapevine forming would be a huge task.

Mom and her sisters would gossip so much. A lot of the old school drama they had going on was lit. The kids would find out about their peer family members, after being confronted by something our mothers had heard. The younger generation of cousins caught on. We did our best to keep our business between us or kept it to ourselves. The older family members likely thought we were boring compared to their generation.

I grappled with the idea of asking my eldest aunt on Moms' side, Mattie. I had to come to terms that I would not care who finds out even if I swore her to secrecy. Before I could build the nerve, she ended up passing. She was one of the sweetest lady's I had ever known.

Our family has this thing of battling illnesses and wanting to be very private about it. There are studies that show sharing the information and having a support system can help with survival rates. Instead of hiding information, they should have been using each other for support the entire time. Her being ill had caught most of us off guard.

At her funeral, I sat next to Mom's other favorite cousin Tina's daughter, Karen. I only saw her twice as an adult. I do not recall seeing her at all as a child. I always found it odd that Mom only went to visit her beloved cousin Tina once when I was 11. She lived fairly close to us on the same side of town, less than 10 minutes away. They would chat on the phone often. Mom told me that she is the person that she stayed with when she first left the south to move to Chicago.

Partly into the service, Karen mentions how much I favored my mom. She said that Mom was a very sweet lady. "I used to watch you all the time when you were little," Karen said. That revelation just shot straight up through me. I did not recall being with her at all. I truly only knew her name through the grapevine and wouldn't recognize her if I saw her on the street. That's how many times I remember being around her.

This revelation hit so hard because the family grapevine had some interesting things to say about Karen and her family. One of the most shocking things was that she was molested by her uncle who always lived with her mother. Apparently, this was an open secret amongst the family. Her children were primarily raised by her mother Tina. Her uncle, the lifelong resident, then goes on to molest Karen's daughter. According to the family grapevine, Karen's daughter has a child by him. The grapevine also reports that both women ended up using drugs to cope.

Aunt Candi's family ended up moving closer to these cousins. Her eldest daughter Carla was chased home by this guy, her own distant cousin. She knew who he was. No one close to us allowed this man to come around.

The first time I saw him, it was at a party. I was a small child, Mom grabbed me in close as we were walking past. He was going in the opposite direction with a chicken bone in his mouth chewing down to the marrow. This is something I still haven't seen anyone else do till this day. He then disappeared behind a door.

I hoped that Karen was just talking. I hope that I was not left with these people and not kept an eye on. This caused me to think if there may have been some willful neglect going on Karen's part, if that man is the culprit.

Due to Karen enduring this ordeal throughout her life, would she allow this pain to be passed along to another child. Was this seen as something that just happened? Maybe this was just a mistake in her eyes.

I am in a prime season of healing. There has been no treatment or support. Something in my spirit would pull me on a subconscious level. This pull was to break me away from this generational curse. Families end up relinquishing the mental state of multiple innocent children just to save one sexual deviant.

It is unfortunate that something as well-intentioned as a girl taking an older man a plate of food can become a dangerous situation. Perhaps the adult woman is attempting to show the girl ways of being submissive or adult woman is just tired. The adult woman should run this task herself. The girl can observe and learn from her. Or that adult male needs to come and get his own food. Everyone acts oblivious when this girl goes missing for some time after she is tasked with taking a plate of food to a bedroom. There should be no going inside the room. Take the food, knock and go.

Holding your children close when that certain person is around is not enough. Stop the whispers of crazy when referring to someone who has the tendency to harm others. Kids are kids, there will be moments that they may wonder off from you. Please share ways to help in avoiding situations of children being in harm's way. Also share ways to obtain effective therapy for individuals with deviant traits.

The best way to avoid this is to not allow them around the children. It is noble to want to save someone from homelessness. However, if this person could cause permanent terror to your children and future generations you need to change your priorities.

These traumatic events caused me to be outwardly shy, introverted and closed in. I can only wonder what parts would have been natural characteristics of mine if this had not happened. People may find this insulated stance as unapproachable or unfriendly. It is true that I avoided attention good or bad.

I always kept things on a positive credible level. My reputation had become so trustworthy that unbeknownst to me, I had become some of my friend's excuse. Whenever they wanted to do something their parents wouldn't allow or to go to a club, they would say that I was going. When they wanted to do something their boyfriends would not normally approve of, they would throw my name in the fray to get instant approval.

I was the good girl with slightly edgy friends. It was a headscratcher to most. People would debate about birds of a feather and could not understand how I maintained my individuality. Some of the elder women waited for my character to turn to have their point proven.

I agree, there are times that I came off as being too nice. That is because I don't care for negativity. I felt that perhaps I can show myself as a positive example of how life can be. Shade, friction and discourse is unnecessary. There is no need display elements of characteristics most people have no use for.

I am nice for the most part, but do not cross me. I know my limits and people should too. The doormat role has never been me. I watch just about everything. I take inventory and act accordingly.

Through my discernment, I do not freely open myself up to everyone. Besides the fact that my foundation of trust was destroyed at an early age, I stay mindful of everyone as an individual in general.

The flipside of being quiet, shy and to yourself, there are people who want in. I have witnessed personal attacks and seen as having antisocial behavior. When all along the basis behind it was repressed trauma. The victims of sexual abuse becomes villainized and victimized again due to changes made on their natural character from traumatic events.

The quiet and shy part of me was basically made from fear. This society does not allow for shyness to exist, especially in an adult. You may be considered rude. Some people do not understand that you can be quiet. Especially, if it does not fit a stereotype that they have accepted to be true of all. Everyone is not loud and seeking attention. Even when you are not seeking attention, being fly will capture attention regardless. I played the background, but I always embraced my fly and stylish ways.

I stayed to myself, to protect myself. If you cannot trust supposed loved ones, who can you trust. My issue was those memories of trauma was long suppressed and hidden in my mind. I destroyed those memories to cope. When Mom did not give me answers I needed I further buried the trauma.

Someone like me would have a hard time with repressed memories getting help. How do you change if you do not know there is a problem nor know the source of the issue? It may help you if you have felt heavy negative energy around you to go ahead and seek credible counseling. This can help you get answers. It can be a start in removing that negative energy or in strategizing a new approach to life.

It may help to have a conversation with family. I have yet to have a conversation with the elders of the family. When the memory first came back, I really wanted to know what answers they possibly had for me. I am 95% sure these predators were family members. I have taken a stance of fence sitting. I no longer care about becoming fodder for the family grapevine. I can only see anger coming from knowing. I also don't want to falsely accuse or become avoidant of the wrong person.

However, I did have a conversation with a couple of my peer relatives about my experiences. I told my longtime friend Faith, first. She encouraged me to ask around and talk to Ben. She was positive he would know something.

I talked to Ben. I asked him if he knows if something had happened to me when I was younger. He said that he didn't think so. I asked him if he remembered helping Mom pull me from Dad's lap, he did remember. I asked if he knew what was behind Mom's evident distain for our stepbrother Don. Ben attributed the distain to Dad owing child support.

But I could not see Mom being angry over child support, that the child cannot control. I realized at that time that Ben may be covering for someone or something, for whatever reason. If he is hiding something in an effort to protect me, it is no longer necessary. I decided not to press him for any more answers.

I talked to two female cousins. We have some degree of code amongst ourselves to not broadcast everything. Although, there are older first cousins born in the late 50's and the 60's. They hung out with our parents. No bones were moved on their part when grown folk business was going on. Many of their kids are around our age. I spoke to Carla first. I would say she is the eldest female of the first cousins of what I consider the younger generation born in the 70's through the 90's.

Carla kept her finger on the pulse of the family. Even though I consider her a part of the younger generation, she had a lot of the old school ways. She knew or had partial information about just about anyone in the family you can think of. She had about a 65% accuracy rate on her information. Partly right in some cases. Keep your grains of salt handy. Immediately after asking Carla if she ever heard of anything happening to me. She had a ready answer. Which took me back a bit.

"My mom said nothing ever happened to you," Carla said swiftly. I was shocked. The fact that this was a conversation between them had taken me back. Carla went on, "my mother told your mom to stop having Uncle Les come around your kids so much."

According to Carla my mother responded to Aunt Candi, "Les would not do anything to hurt her kids." My mom could be stubborn at times. It was interesting since he was already on my suspect list.

It had been suspected that some inappropriate acts were committed by Uncle Les. Les was in the eldest half of my grandmother's bunch of 12 children. My Aunt took great precaution with her kids whenever he was around. She put her kids on notice to avoid him. He was not welcome in her house.

I had no idea my Aunt had this avoidant relationship with Uncle Les. I was surprised that neither her nor her kids went to his funeral when he passed away. No one ever gave a reason why. I didn't go because I had minor surgery on my arm around that time.

CHAPTER 13

MISINTERPRETATION OF MEN

For the longest time, I never knew that men had feelings. It is not that I went around hurting feelings. There was a time not so long ago, when there was a shunning of men who expressed their emotions. As far back as I can remember, I saw masculine men leading with testosterone. Men who experienced the toughest things in life would face things heads up, eye to eye. A man crying is something you would be hard pressed to witness. Their voices were deep and commanded respect. They did not publicly display their need for love. However, they would openly show their desire for sex.

I have had my own experiences to show me who men are. Then, there is a view of who I interpreted men to be through mainstream media and propaganda. The softer side of men being shown in the mainstream today is something new. Males who would show the slightest signs of giving in to emotions were told to be strong and suck it up (||). Strong men challengers and athletes were common on the silver screen. White collar pencil pushers to blue collar workers had wives along with a core family at home.

I adore men. Although, I don't like all of their ways. Whatever my view had been conditioned to see, that love has always been there. Even at times when I was not able to fully express those feelings. Perhaps, my vision became trained on seeing passive male traits such as being caviler, nonchalant, mean spirited or having a disregard for the feelings of others. This was my process of thinking so much so that I would see it in all men. I thought they had no true capacity to love, which in turn led me to believe that they had no feelings.

In any case, all men cannot be thrown into one box. Of course, different people can carry similarities. Even with similarities, that does not mean two people are the same. Identical twins carrying the same DNA are still two individuals. You may even attract the same type of mate over time, without thinking twice about why you are attracting the same type of mate.

I always knew what I wanted in life. When it came to relationships, I wanted to be married around 20 years old to a respectable man with upstanding moral character who is also a protector and provider. I wanted at least three kids, all in my twenties. Fielding out a suitor variety was not in my plan. Mainly because I was not that social butterfly. While growing out of my shyness, meeting a bunch of new people was not ideal for me.

In my relationships, sometimes that connection just was not there. Even when there was a connection, both parties may have not been ready or not on the same page. Some people take joy in spreading themselves around or sowing their wild oats. One thing that we often forget to take into consideration, your plans may not always come into fruition. Especially when your plans require cooperation from others.

The gift of discernment can screen through a true gentleman and someone putting on a gentleman act. They have all the right things to say. They show you only what you need to see. Their timing is perfect. They will have you all pegged up, down to a science.

Are you dealing with a gentleman or a conman? One truly means what he says and does. The other has a hidden agenda. By the time you get through the crux of that agenda, it is often too late. There is nothing more heartbreaking than over-committing to someone with a fraudulent heart.

Hidden misdeeds can show on the surface, even when it goes unspoken. The energy carries. It's that one thing you cannot seem to put your finger on, but you know it is there. Especially, when your gut feeling speaks to you.

The act of rape sends off many subliminal messages to the victim. You often hear that incidents of rape are not necessarily about the sex. It is about power. It is unfortunate that I had to go through something so painful, sickening and immoral at such an early age. I had to engage in mental gymnastics with myself to try and destroy the memory just to cope. But it was never fully destroyed. It reappeared later in life as a repressed memory.

There were encounters of other slight violations of space and body. When a person is moving too fast on a date, you tend to become wiser each time you go out. Know when to exit if you have to end things early. You never know when a person's mind has given themselves the green light to get handsy. Whenever a person takes it upon themselves to violate your space and body, this indicates a lack of respect.

Growing up, I would normally get distracted by the pull your hair guy. Or the coping free feels guy. Even the snatch your snacks guy. Not to mention the splash water on you guy.

My friends and I would walk to the nearby strip mall about a half mile away two or three times a week. We had three route options to get there. We could go straight up our street. But once you cross the street there is a section that was desolate. The old factories sat there a little too quietly. It was a straight shot, but we rarely took this option. There were two main roads that sat closer together than most in the city, Kedzie and Homan. Taking the main roads were for our protection by providing better visibility. We took Kedzie just about all the time.

One day, we decided to take Homan to the mall. Homan was a little bit out of the way. It was like adding another couple of blocks to the walk. But it provided better access to a nice BBQ spot and a free-standing store that sat on the corner that we would frequent.

While Kedzie had active factories on along the strip. Homan had homes on along the street that we rarely paid attention to by it being a two-way street. A bunch of teenage guys none of us knew grabbed each one of us and threw us into a full blast fire hydrant on this busy two-way street. We could not see or breathe. We did not know these guys from anywhere. Maybe they were grabbing anything moving and this was their version of fun.

When I would draw this type of negative attention people would tell me, he's just doing that because he likes you. He just wants your attention. So, these guys are doing things to make me despise them instead of doing things in a caring way to get my attention? It made no sense to me.

It would have been nice to attract the sweet gestures guy. Instead of taking something offer something. He could have gotten one out of the 25 cent bubble gum machines for all I cared. Do something if you are having trouble expressing yourself in a positive manner.

Perhaps most guys saw me as hard to reach because I was so quiet, shy and off to myself. That anxious energy was hard to break through. Guys would go through my friends to reach me instead of talking to me straight up and direct. My friends pranked too much, so I never trusted them when they came to me about what a guy said. Were these guys expecting me to come back to them and strike up a conversation? That would never happen. I did not need my friends to be my mouthpiece either. I just needed the right approach.

My carefree nonchalant lifestyle may have seemed impenetrable. Peace of mind is immensely valued. I may come off as though I am not deeply emotionally entrenched on the surface. Particularly because I do not express my feelings much. The 'I love you's were not dished around often in my childhood. I did not think much of it back then. I knew that my family cared. They showed it in various ways. Or maybe my calm nature was seen as a storm was a brewing. People seem afraid to approach you when they cannot get an instantly read on your purpose and personality.

Generally, men provide balance to a woman's life and vice versa. Anxious energy can exacerbate imbalance. There is nothing wrong with submission to a mate who can lead. So long as, your mate has a plan and good intentions.

There was a time I thought men had all the answers. This was my frame of thought just about all my life. My experience with irrational men with illogical actions caused me to think that men were incredibly complex. Especially when they would do things that totally worked against their benefit. Violation of someone's space and body benefits no one, not even the person seeking temporary gratification.

The truth is men are incredibly simple. Don't overthink things. Your mate may not always live up to your expectations. Or you may not measure up to your mate. Basic needs may be overlooked or go unmet. Think visual and surface when it comes to men. It is impossible to gauge a person's character, mind or heart at first sight. In most cases, that is the last thing on their mind when you attract a man's eyesight.

The more appealing you are, men may have more of an expectation to be manipulated. It could be the reason why they cower or run when they feel things are going too good. Just as a peacock shows their feathers some men attain flashy things to attract women. These women may seek out flashy things as well. There is upkeep involved. Bigger, higher, more and more expensive. What is the basis of this relationship if the money runs dry?

What happens when her attention does not require a bunch of material things? She is beautiful, smart, fun to be around and everything you ever wanted. And she really likes you for you. What is her problem, right? Why you? Is this real? Do you accept her and love her? Or do you let her go and continuing to search for the never ending unknown.

I have had relationships fail because the guy felt like he did not measure up. This happens at some point after I am fully emotionally invested. I would hear, "you deserve better." I would only wish that they had known that sooner than I began investing my emotions. I will not refute that. Apparently, you know something about yourself that I have not discovered yet. Or there is something about you that does not mesh with who I am.

I thought they were good enough. For the most part, they all shared some components of being hard working, college educated, veterans, ambitious, handy, business minded and handsome. They were young but, not fully established. I was looking to build because neither was I, fully established. Just because I do not complain much or come off as needy does not mean they were not wanted or needed.

Maybe, I was focusing on their potential. The traits my exes had were workable to build a strong foundation for the future. Most of them had great character. The pretenders even acted like they did until they broke character and could no longer play the role. The "you deserve better" line wore on me after a while. I reached my breaking point to where I got tired of experiencing this. So, I fell back from dating. It will happen when it is meant to happen. The right one will know and understand me. Far be it for me to force anything on anyone. That true love thing. I will know it when I see it. When he comes, I am there in genuine kind.

The funny thing is the guys I dated also seemed to come up with the same nickname, 'Cool Ass Mo'. None of these guys knew each other. Let me place those pieces together, 'Cool Ass Mo deserves better'. Interesting. Especially for someone who did not choose lowly men. Most of the guys I dated did not drink. If they drank it was socially on occasion. They were not drug addicts at any point. I hoped to grow with someone close to my age. Our only faults were being young and unestablished financially. I wanted someone my age because I used to get embarrassed when people would mislabel my father as my granddad.

I have many positive attributes to be proud of. Unfortunately, positive attributes are not celebrated in some communities in the same manner they are celebrated by the rest of the world. I may have been viewed as a good fit to be some man's trophy. Like a woman keeping up a role with no real connection. A kept woman.

The young men I dated feared that 'the money man' was coming. A more financially stable man. I had no interest in being bought. If my heart is with you, it is with you. I like a good guy with high moral values and true good character. I did not want to end up breaking up with some guy for him to come back and show out on me to repossess his trinkets. I love nice things. But things are not important in a sense that I would do anything for them. I will find the means to obtain it myself if it is that important to me.

There is a whole segment of women who exist that live for the trinkets and things. The same way things are given to build someone up. These things can be taken away in a whim when trying to destroy that person. I have never been up for that game.

In all honesty, that little nickname and advice should have been my cue to step it up. Seek out a more stable and mature man to dispel all that financial insecurity. One less hurdle to get over in a relationship. Instead, I stepped back from dating. Imbalanced relationships are exhausting. If one person in the relationship is forward thinking and marriage minded but the other wants to stay in same place something will break.

Some of my ex's have apologized for years after breaking up. That is fine. Just think before you act. This could help to lessen the guilt. After a breakup, I do not feel as though I am owed anything. Although, closure is always good for both parties. Apologizing years later always made me curious. I have no idea why they would do this. The reason and timing were always unclear.

I never had to fight and scratch to get back with an ex. I never needed an intervention from a, 'No, but I love him' moment. We parted ways amicably. No pushing and prodding necessary. We know where we stand. I would however stretch for the right guy who also stretches for me. They say you can't get something from nothing. They also say nothing ventured, nothing gained. It does not matter who 'they' are. Do not get caught up in the 'they' but catch the message.

Disrespect can only play out for so long. People can show you their true character to the point of no return to your good graces. If a person violates you, they should not be able to come floating back with ease. You have to value you before anyone else can. If you like it over there, stay over there. If you like it over here, show some gratitude.

Taking on the challenge of dissecting my life in relation to everyone, particularly men brings me clarity. Experience brings wisdom. Assessing and examining my life may bring insight to you to better understand yourself. I believe that I have a better understanding of myself and how I relate to men. I see that I was wrong in some of my ways. Not in such a bad way. More transparency and communication on my part would have helped me immensely. Finding out what held me back from giving what was needed was a relief. This is an internal battle that I had no idea even existed. Now that I know, it ends here.

My understanding is to always do better. Challenge yourself to the best this world has to offer. It is amazing how many things can be turned around. Bad things being celebrated as good. Negative things get the reaction. Positive feedback falls flat. In certain communities, women are berated for furthering their education, taking on challenging careers and creating entrepreneurial endeavors. An insecure man can take it as a knock on his presence. What part of self-improvement screams stay away? If anything, she can add to what you have to offer. Believing in each other and building together is possible.

It is not reasonable to sit still in hopes of someone coming along to pick up your life. This is especially true with high divorce rates. If that relationship were to end, a person can be left stuck. No practical skills moving forward can leave a person lost with nowhere to turn. The cycle continues by looking for the next person to come along to pick up their life. You may or may not luck up.

Having someone who can help you build should not be a threat. See them as a partner in empire building. Let me be blessed enough to have someone of high moral character who can bring excess and abundance into my life. I am stashing and keeping it.

TRUTH BEING BONDAGE

Then again, I may still have a misinterpretation of men. Breaking through the negativity of what I had experienced early on in life is still a process. It was unrealistic to expect me to turn out to become this outwardly loving being. With edification, we learn and grow every day. I hope the tide has turned to gaining pure love and understanding.

CHAPTER 14

LIFE IS AN EXPERIENCE, YOU MUST BE PRESENT TO LIVE

Life is too short to let trauma rule over you. In no way shape or form do I claim to be trained in therapy, a Doctor of Medicine or a psychiatrist. All I have are my life experiences. I share my story to free it from myself. Maybe sharing my story can help free others. Perhaps, you or someone you know can relate.

Take time out for yourself to figure out how you need to show up in your life. Falling into a daily routine is easy, especially when each move is considered necessary. Take care of yourself. The part we automatically deem necessary often comes in last.

We all want to have the fullest experience of life that we can have. A full experience is defined differently for each person. One person may hold value to one thing that could mean absolutely nothing to the next person. It is up to you of what you value and hold dear to your heart.

In times where we fall short of our goals or expectations, often we become hard on ourselves. If you are not showing up fully in your life, figure out the source of the void. It is harmful to diminish yourself or allow others to diminish your works. It is best that you recognize your energy and what you need to do to start enjoying your life. Start with appreciation.

Realistically, life is full of twists and turns. There is no guarantee at any point your life will be perfect. All we can do is make the best of what we have, work to obtain what we need and take care of what we can control. Being alive is one thing. Putting in that effort to living your life is another.

You can minimize the twists and turns in life by staying away from wickedness and trouble. Do not keep close company with people who have troublesome ways. You don't need the complexities these relationships bring.

Try to recognize when you are dealing with liars and shallow people. This can save you a lot of time, headaches and heartaches. Early on, this person may have lied on their career, a car that was not their car or embellish their position in life. All these things are done to enter your life by gaining favor. You may be flattered by someone going to such extremes to impress you. It is not so endearing when a person consistently lies. Once you find that first lie and stay, it is an approval and opens the door to more deceit.

It does not take long to recognize a shallow person either. It may be that certain someone who is not really there for you. They like what they see on the outside and they could care less about what is on the inside. Especially when the best of you lies beneath the surface. They may try a parroting technique. They mimic or repeat things you have said with no sincerity. This shell of a person will eventually grow tired of the farce. Essentially, they were just catering to your ego to stick around.

On the other hand, there are some relationships that exist only by shallow means. Both parties are willing and aware of their position. The transactional relationship is about sex and money. They get what they came to get with no strings attached. Some people want the shiniest jewel. It can cost you.

Some people will drain their pockets down flat to keep up appearances with someone who wants to stay in a luxury field trip fantasy. Some people will put up with any standard of character so long as they can hold on to the aesthetics. If that is what you are signing up for, what is for you, is for you. What's your price and what will it cost you in the end?

I have always been a proponent against wasting energy. It always seemed like a time waster to engage in simple arguments. Should you engage to show that you care and that they are worth your time? A person may create conflicts to test of your action to see how to move forward with you in conflict.

Be awakened to the facts of your routine. If your routine is not beneficial to you, change it. Picture and plan the type of life you want. The things you really want in life, will take action and movement on your part. Keep it positive. Take in wisdom and knowledge and apply it. Be for you. When God is with you who can be against you.

Before attaching yourself in a relationship, find and figure yourself out first. Brighten your future. Know what you like, what you want, always put forth the effort and continue to do so.

If you are single and dating has taken a backseat. While you are patiently waiting in the process, be active in your self-improvement. You will be in a much better position to share your world with someone.

Fractures in life deserve the time for repair. Healing takes some time. That does not mean stop living. Keep going and be reasonable. Take a couple of months for yourself, don't overlap relationships just to keep repeating history.

I enjoy life whether being still, being out on the town or traveling. When you find a bit of bliss in the things you enjoy, life gets easier. I take solace in knowing that I don't have to be everything to everybody. You cannot control everyone's perception either. It is best to just be yourself. Take it, love it or leave it. Contorting yourself to fit in with others will burn you out. That is no way to live.

It is an interesting journey to travel to different cultural corners. It does not take a trip around the world to experience this. You can go as little as 50 to 500 miles away from home to experience nuances that are totally different than what you see on a day-to-day basis. A cultural difference is not limited to what you experience in the people. You can experience differences in things like local artistic expression or cuisine.

Traveling can create a new learning opportunity. You can learn more about yourself just by observing new things and comparing it to what you are accustomed to. You may land in a place where the people are more receptive to you. They approach you to strike up a conversation. This may be a general cultural expression of the area you visit, or maybe you are a newcomer. The people are generally friendly and open.

I acknowledge and admit there were times that I was not totally present in my relationships. Unfortunately, an underline feeling of anxiety had followed me. Being guarded and watchful over everything and everybody was daunting.

Although, I will remain watchful. I can let my guard down a tad. Bottling yourself in negative encounters or what else may happen has to stop. Change up that mindset. The worst is behind me. The best road is ahead. Claim it!

OUTLOOK & DISPOSITION

My outlook on life has always been positive and optimistic. I appreciate my parents for helping to guide me in the direction of positivity. My outlook has always been my fuel to keep going. It makes each day feel anew. Boredom rarely takes hold of me. There is plenty out there for me to learn, experience and various aspects of life to grow in. I put forth effort every day to amplify positivity.

I am a fair person and I value others who deal in a similar fashion. You make life easier on yourself and others when you do the right things.

That pressing feeling to run to escape the brokenness, can stop now. Everything is alright. I have outrun the past. It is time to set my own pace.

I vow to express my feelings and thoughts more. I cannot leave it to someone else's imagination to fill in the blanks. No one knows your heart like you do. You know what appeases your mind. It is a valuable shift when you leave no room for doubt. No two people think the same or interpret things the same way.

You must give relationships some direction. I used to think along the lines of if you let a person know of your intent for a more serious relationship, you would run them off. Plainly put, if they are quick to run off, they were not there for the right reasons in the first place. It is better they run off now than later. No one wants a ciphering opportunist budding up against them for some momentary gain.

Be upfront about where you want to be. Also be upfront with your companions about your goals and placement in their life. It is best to hear and know the truth.

Placing relationships in a higher priority in my life may be a healthy move. Attracting positive relationships and arrangements can enhance your life. It is up to you to put forth the effort control how you use your energy. A role can only be played for so long. A genuine person will not change. A person playing a role will stop or come out of their character eventually.

If the person is not on Broadway earning a check, they cannot uphold that character for long. Why would anyone want to come into a relationship that way? A fault of mine had been taking on characters. I could sense when a person was not being genuine with me. When they got major co-signs from my family and friends, I grew deeper into the relationships. Perhaps they saw something amazing I didn't see. Afterall, the recommendation came from people I love and care about.

If I had my way with the universe aligning, a mental and spiritual connection would have taken place early on with my soulmate. Ideally, I would have married somewhere between 18-22. When I was young and had little concept of money, I desired the stability of marriage along with a small tribe of children. I could care less for variety and all the twists and turns that comes with dating and meeting new people. It requires a certain level of people person to successfully manage the dating scene.

Marriage was not something I ever pressed for. There are a couple of people I would have liked to build a life with. And one I would have taken a chance with but, part of me knows that it would have been pure struggle the whole time. Unfortunately, no one ever informed me about the male ego. It requires a lot of attention. I can respect that.

Aside from the male ego, narcissism is something we hear a lot about these days. It was not a commonly defined term or identified action when I first started dating. When I experienced this, I just thought people were just acting out and they would go back to being their normal self. It actually was them breaking character and taking on a whole new role. Unbearable and obnoxious is the best way to describe it.

The only thing that was consistent were the apologies. They would apologize many times over throughout the years. I hold no ill feelings toward them. It's just hard to tell when they are dealing in true sincerity.

There is the first man I believe who would have been a good fit as a husband or life partner. We were like minded in seeking knowledge and our desire to build wealth. We were in our early twenties. He had already done a tour of duty in the service.

Oddly enough, he reminded me of my mother due to being akin to an old soul, laid-back and firm. I could talk to him about anything. There are so many nice things I wanted to do for him, but I held back. I really cared for him. He expressed that he did not want to be in an exclusive relationship. I never held back my feeling for him. I always stopped short of telling him that I loved him. Whenever I needed him to be there for me, he was there.

I came to the point where I had to know why he did not want to move further. I asked, "what's going on, do you think that you are too good for me?" He said, "maybe you are too good for me. You deserve someone better than me. If it is meant to be, I can let you go and you will come back to me."

"So basically, if you let a dog roam. He will find his way home. That's what you are saying?" I replied (sarcasm).

I backed up further from him. He was not done playing the field. He even revealed years later that he pretended to be in a relationship with another woman. I did not ask him to go into the details of why he did this. I immediately thought it was a buffer. That way he would not feel pressure from me for a relationship.

This started to become a common theme. You deserve better, is what they would tell me. After so long, I almost wanted that breakup fight. At least I would have a clue about what I am doing wrong. Except I get told that things are too much like right and I deserve someone better. My only fault is seeing potential in them, that perhaps they did not see in themselves.

In my early twenties I was of the mindset that if his career is taking off first, my mate would handle things on my behalf while I finish school. I would do the same for him if he was in school or taking up a trade. We could have backed each other up like that and vice versa. If one of us desired to start a business, the other could handle the everyday household financial obligations or join in with the operation of the business until things get off the ground. I always wanted a supportive situation like that. Instead, the relationships were counterproductive.

Dad let me know that I had things a little better than most young folks my age. He brought this up so that I would be grateful and to make me aware of any dissention that could occur in that existence. This discord can almost be expected among other females. My true friends never gave me any issues. Most of the issues were with guys. Their favorite line was, "it must be nice." Whenever I heard this line, I knew things were pretty much on the verge of being over.

In my eyes there is no need to compete. I don't care if you have more money or whatever than me. Let's work together and see how we can grow. Listening to morning radio shows back then, men would complain about their girlfriends and wives not adding income to the household. So, I was taken aback when guys seemed to have issues with what a woman bringing her own finances to the table.

I have always been open to marriage only if it is right for me. My initial goal for marriage was to create a family. I am past that being the primary basis for marriage.

Did I figure all this out too late? Perhaps, better late than never. I enjoy my alone time as well. However, I would like to enhance my space and time by building and strengthening relationships. Strong connections are critical in maintaining relationships.

Thriving relationships is a desire of mine. I must be mindful to enhance my companions, friends and associates' space and time as well by adding value in different ways. It takes time to nurture people and relationships. We should embrace the time it takes.

This journey of reflecting on the past when it comes to family, relationships and how I have approached things in my life has brought things full circle. There is greatness in gaining understanding. It was a must to pull from the past to make myself aware of the present and bring insight into the future. As I reflect on the relationships critical in building my foundation. I would be remiss not to mention the best lessons learned from my core family members, Mom, Dad and Ben.

Before I start on my core family. My relationship with my peer cousins, is a special one. I saved my cousins from jumping all at once. This was not intentional. We had gone to a home family gathering in Bolingbrook, IL. After we ate, one of our relatives invited us to hang out at a local park. We drove down to the location. The park was more like a forest preserve.

We were all entering early adulthood. We had a big kid moment. There was at least ten of us. We just took off running and laughing. There was no particular game, just being truly young and free. Then, I looked ahead. Faintly I thought, that looks like an express way sign. It appeared to be below where we were running. I looked again. I yelled, "STOP"! I stood still yelling STOP over and over until everyone stopped. There were no warning signs. No barriers were anywhere to be found. We had no idea that we were even on an elevation. The park had an abrupt cliff where the interstate exchange lay below. Everyone heard the warning. No one was harmed. There is a youthfulness that comes out amongst us anytime we come together. This bond has been a positive key factor in my life.

The best lessons learned from Mom was instilling that no one is any better than you and don't act as if I am better than anyone else. This is why I treat everyone fairly, so long as they don't show me otherwise. She instilled that I could do anything that I set my mind to.

The reality is, street life was only steps away from our front door. There was no reason to sugarcoat or act oblivious to the facts. She made that apart of her spiel. She told me to be careful of anyone who may try to turn me on to drugs. They may say "just try it this one time, it won't hurt you."

Be aware of pimps. This is anyone trying to have you go out on the street to make money for them. Also, watch out for any man trying to put his hands on me and telling me he is doing it because he loves me. Do not stay! Get away from his ass! That's not love! Do not let any person put their hands on you and tell you that's love!

Mom passed away a few months after my 16th birthday. She fell ill in the previous two years. We never had the chance to have a dialog about the attack I experienced in my early years. That is the one thing I wish we could have had a real conversation about. In my belief, she did not withhold information from me because it was unimportant. She did not want to face the reality of the hard truth nor disrupt our lives. I have years to live beyond childhood. This truth disrupted my life even though this reality laid dormant in me. I was extremely guarded in close and intimate relationships.

Best lessons learned from Dad was about money and credit. He never got personal about how to conduct myself or what to expect in relationships. He allowed me to accept credit cards at age 17. I had a friend who was a year ahead of me. She graduated high school the previous year and enrolled full-time at Northwestern University. She took me on a tour of the campus. We stopped in a student center where there were two tables set up for credit cards. We both put in credit applications. I adjusted my birthday a bit just to see what happens. I was eventually sent two credit cards with $1000 limits on each.

I thought Dad would be upset with me for doing this. I was still and minor and had not started my part-time job yet. Dad said, "You may as well start building your credit now. Do not charge these cards up. Just buy what you need. Try to pay these cards off by the due date. If you cannot do that, at least make sure you pay the minimum balance. Pay them down because the interest will continue to build, even when there is no minimum balance due."

When Ben and I became teenagers, I did not understand why Dad would have us write out all the bills every month. We filled out the bill slip, envelope and the money orders. He said that he preferred our handwriting better. Ben does have some of the best handwriting you would want to see. But I believe Dad wanted us to get in the habit of staying on top of our bills when we got older to prevent credit issues later.

The angst was finally broken between Dad and I, after I turned 18. Dad was installing a sport accessory on my car. I asked him a question about tires attempting to strike up a conversation. He got into his usual fussy mode when all he really had to do was give me a yes or no or talk regular. I took this as an opportunity.

In the past, I would let him fuss or leave. As a kid, I showed respect and did not talk back. This time I was an adult. It was now time to address this. I told him, I asked you a simple question you don't have to yell at me. Everything got quiet. He was still working on the car. I ended up leaving the garage. I had no idea what would come of this interaction.

What came of me addressing how he delt with me verbally resulted in him never addressing me in a fussy tone ever again. It was so satisfying. We gained a mutual respect for each other. I could finally talk to him. He ended up becoming one of my closest confidants. I never saw that coming.

I know adults in their 30's, 40's and 50's who are still afraid to confront a parent about the manner in which their parents address them. The conversation doesn't have to turn into an argument. Speak in your normal tone. People hold on to somethings forever. Just hoping that one day a person change does not work. Most times people do not know how you feel. Especially when you let things slide for so long. It's never too late. Make it right.

Best lesson learned from Ben is to pay attention. Know who is who and what is what. Know where your value lies. Know that you are at the helm of your life. In my opinion, he always wanted to win at something, no matter what it was. Those mischievous ways were a hinderance. When everyone says 'no', whatever you do... don't do that. He would be the one who dared to go where other people have gone to no avail. Ben would be the one to say the heck with that. I am going in for the win.

You don't have to be the top or the chosen one. Choose yourself and love yourself enough to make the right decisions. Do the right things for you. Do not sabotage your life by getting in your own way. You deserve happiness, yes you!

As a bonus, the best lesson learned from one of my stepbrothers is, "never put nothing past what a man would do." It was just that simple, yet that deep. He repeated the sentiment in our phone conversation about four times. Point taken. Bar none.

About the Author

Mo Abbie is only beginning her journey into the field of writing. Sharing this deeply personal history was difficult, but necessary. Perhaps the reader may find healing or a better path from any lessons learned. Mo has interests in healthy lifestyles and land development. For any updates, blogs and future projects please visit www.forti-fiedone.com. Thank you for reading.

www.ingramcontent.com/pod-product-compliance
Lightning Source LLC
LaVergne TN
LVHW090054080526
838200LV00082B/1